SHARE GROUP TRAINING

Part 1: Building Bridges Opening Hearts

By Ralph W. Neighbour, Jr.

Touch Outreach Ministries

This book is the first of three in a series.
The titles of the next two are:

- **Building Groups, Opening Hearts**
- **Building Awareness, Opening Hearts**

Illustrations by Joe McKeever

With love, for Barry and Renee Oswald

© 1991 • TOUCH Outreach Ministries, Inc.
All Rights Reserved

ISBN 1-880828-63-4

Available from:
TOUCH Outreach Ministries
P.O. Box 19888 • Houston, TX 77224-9888, USA
Telephone (281) 497-7901 • Fax: (281) 497-0904
Website: www.touchusa.org

Printed by BAC Printers
Singapore

CONTENTS

HOW TO USE THIS BOOK

1. Attend the MINISTRY OUTREACH WEEKEND, and experience the "Description of Your Ministry" section with your fellow Share Group team members.

2. Remove the Bible memory verses from the centerfold, cut them out, and begin to memorize two verses each week.

3. Set a specific time and place to meet daily with your Lord. Use the material in this book to guide you during these times.

4. Do one day's work each day for five days. Do one Unit each week.

5. During each week, complete the Practical Activity assignment. Be prepared to share your written report during the Equipping Time when you attend your cell group.

6. Use **"THE TEAM SHARES"** pages when your team meets together during Cell Group Equipping Times.

THE CELL GROUP AND ITS OUTREACH MINISTRIES

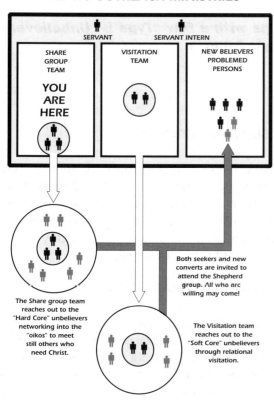

SERVANT   SERVANT INTERN

SHARE GROUP TEAM

YOU ARE HERE

VISITATION TEAM

NEW BELIEVERS PROBLEMED PERSONS

The Share group team reaches out to the "Hard Core" unbelievers networking into the "oikos" to meet still others who need Christ.

Both seekers and new converts are invited to attend the Shepherd group. All who are willing may come!

The Visitation team reaches out to the "Soft Core" unbelievers through relational visitation.

MINISTRY OUTREACH WEEKEND

What Is The Next Part Of Your Journey?

You have learned to reach "Type A" unbelievers during the last stage of your journey into ministry. Now, you will be equipped to build bridges to the most neglected people: the "Type B," or "Hard Core," unbelievers. For every "Type A" unbeliever, there are several thousand "Type B's" who live without hope, without Christ—*and with little possibility that anyone will share the good news of God's love with them!* Our cell group church is determined to reach these untouched people. You are being equipped to know how to do that. In the years to come, you will find you have been equipped to help many who are blind to Christ's love receive spiritual sight.

You are now part of a "Share Group" team. Typically, your team will be made up of three persons, or two married couples. Your goal is to develop a trust relationship between yourself and two "Type B" unbelievers, making it possible for you to demonstrate your faith by your life and your spoken witness.

Perhaps your first question is, "What is a Share Group?" And, probably your next question is, "Am I capable of bringing two persons with me to participate in one?" This first booklet is designed to answer those questions for you.

YOUR JOURNEY WILL BE IN THREE PHASES . . .

First, you'll spend some time developing closer relationships with a few "Type B" Unbelievers. (We'll learn more about their characteristics in the pages that follow.)

The purpose of your journey is to reach those who have no interest in spiritual matters. Satan has blinded their eyes, made them deaf to the voice of God, and has directed them to waste their lives on matters of little consequence. Reaching them for Christ is the greatest challenge a Christian will ever face. Once you have experienced this ministry, you will never be the same person again!

PHASE 1: BUILDING BRIDGES

The materials in this book are designed to help you as your Team is *BUILDING BRIDGES* to Type "B" unbelievers who will be invited to attend your Share Group. Developing bonds of friendship with those who need Christ must precede the launching of this special group.

PHASE 2: BUILDING GROUPS

After you have learned how to build bridges to Type "B" unbelievers, your Team will form a 10-week Share Group with Type "B" unbelievers. You will then use *BUILDING GROUPS,* the second book in this series. That book will help you minister as you go through your first experience with cell group evangelism.

PHASE 3: BUILDING AWARENESS

After the 10-week Share Group is over, the most important phase of all takes place. You and your team will then concentrate on getting acquainted with the *families and friends* of those who attended your Share Group. By expanding the awareness of these people, the message of Christ's love will draw some to Him.

The first part of this book is designed to be used in a MINISTRY OUTREACH WEEKEND. You and your Team will share this experience together. Its pages will help you grasp the scope of your ministry.

You are then provided with materials to use each day—five days each week— as you build bridges to those who will enter your Share Group.

ARE YOU READY? SHALL WE BEGIN?

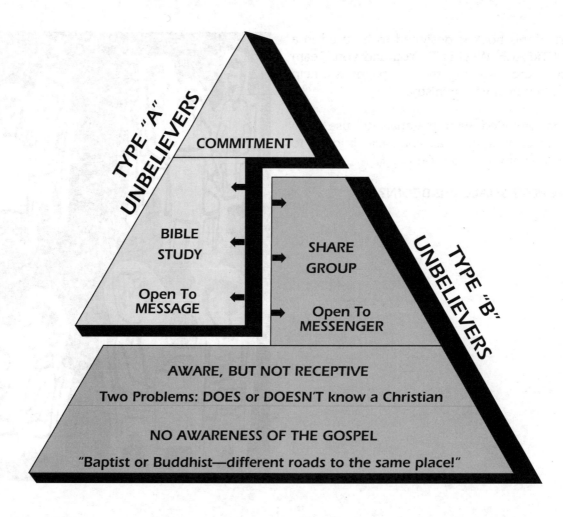

TYPE "A" UNBELIEVERS

TYPE "B" UNBELIEVERS

COMMITMENT

BIBLE STUDY

Open To MESSAGE

SHARE GROUP

Open To MESSENGER

AWARE, BUT NOT RECEPTIVE

Two Problems: DOES or DOESN'T know a Christian

NO AWARENESS OF THE GOSPEL

"Baptist or Buddhist—different roads to the same place!"

THERE ARE TWO TYPES OF UNBELIEVERS

Type "A" Unbelievers:

They are the "Like us" people—easily reached.

CHARACTERISTICS:

- They will attend church services.
- They already believe in the God of the Bible.
- They accept the Bible as true.
- They may have had a church membership in the past.
- They are searching for something, and have visited a Celebration.
- They may not have all the "pieces of the puzzle" in place, as far as Christian knowledge is concerned.
- Bible study, and explaining the plan of salvation to them, are appropriate activities.

YOU HAVE ALREADY LEARNED HOW TO SHARE CHRIST AS YOU PERFORMED THE MINISTRY OF THE GUIDEBOOK, "KNOCKING ON DOORS, OPENING HEARTS."

Type "B" Unbelievers:

They are the "Hard To Reach" people.

CHARACTERISTICS:

- They have seldom attended a church.
- They have no desire to do so.
- They may know little about God.
- They don't know the Bible is a special book.
- They don't understand Jesus is God.
- They are not searching for Christian truth.
- They have few "pieces of the puzzle" in place.
- Bible study, or explaining the plan of salvation, is not yet appropriate for them.
- There must first be time to develop relationships, exposing them to the Christ who lives in you.

YOU WILL NOW LEARN HOW TO REACH OUT TO THEM AS YOU COMPLETE THE THREE "SHARE GROUP TRAINING" MODULES.

LIST BELOW THE NAMES OF TWO "TYPE A" UNBELIEVERS YOU KNOW:

_____

_____

LIST BELOW THE NAMES OF TWO "TYPE B" UNBELIEVERS YOU KNOW:

_____

_____

SMALL GROUP TIME: (6 MINUTES)

**SHARE YOUR LIST
WITH THE MEMBERS
OF YOUR TEAM.
PRAY TOGETHER FOR
THE LORD
TO GIVE YOU
OPENINGS TO
REACH THEM.**

SHARE GROUPS
AS A LIFESTYLE

Being a part of a Share Group team is more of a lifestyle than a project. It means you will take the initiative to help others move one step closer to Christ than they have ever been before.

There's a scripture that describes this process. Let's think about what it teaches us . . .

Again Jesus began to teach by the lake . . . "Listen! A farmer went out to sow his seed. As he was scattering the seed, some fell along the path, and the birds came and ate it up. Some fell on rocky places, where it did not have much soil. It sprang up quickly, because the soil was shallow. But when the sun came up, the plants were scorched, and they withered because they had no root. Other seed fell among thorns, which grew up and choked the plants, so that they did not bear grain. Still other seed fell on good soil. It came up, grew and produced a crop, multiplying thirty, sixty, or even a hundred times." Then Jesus said, "He who has ears to hear, let him hear." When he was alone, the Twelve and the others around him asked him about the parables. He told them . . . "The farmer sows the word. Some people are like seed along the path, where the word is sown. As soon as they hear it, Satan comes and takes away the word that was sown in them. Others, like seed sown on rocky places, hear the word and at once receive it with joy. But since they have no root, they last only a short time. When trouble or persecution comes because of the word, they quickly fall away. Still others, like seed sown among thorns, hear the word; but the worries of this life, the deceitfulness of wealth and the desires for other things come in and choke the word, making it unfruitful. Others, like seed sown on good soil, hear the word, accept it, and produce a crop —thirty, sixty or even a hundred times what was sown."

WHAT IS THE PROCESS?

Phase One: Cultivating

". . .people are like seed along the path . . ."

Jesus said that the soil in His illustration represented human hearts. We must speak to the unbeliever's heart through cultivating a relationship. Your contact with an unbeliever will probably be the very first time he or she has ever become close to a Christian.

Phase Two: Sowing

". . . The farmer sows the Word . . ."

God's word speaks to the unbeliever. We communicate His love first by our relationship, later by scripture. Most "Type B" unbelievers think being a Christian is accepting a set of beliefs, or behaving according to a set of standards. They don't have any way of knowing that we live in a *relationship* with a *Person*—Jesus!

Phase Three: Harvesting

". . . other seed fell on good soil. It came up, grew and produced a crop, multiplying thirty, sixty, or even a hundred times . . ."

Not all of those we will work with will come to Christ and receive Him as Lord, *but some will!* We have no way of knowing when we sow the Word whether it is falling on good soil, rocky soil, wayside soil, or thorn-filled soil. We must leave the results of our ministry in God's hands. *He only asks us to be faithful!*

How Much Time Should I Spend In Each Phase?

There's no pattern that we can set which will insure a person will accept Christ. However, there's a general misunderstanding about the relative importance of the three phases. The illustration on the facing page indicates the approach most of us take:

14

THE MORE TIME

WE SPEND

CULTIVATING,

THE GREATER

WILL BE THE

HARVEST!

WE ARE TO BE SERVANTS TO THE PEOPLE IN "OIKOSES"

Acts 16:31: They replied, "Believe in the Lord Jesus, and you will be saved—you and your household (Oikos)."

An "OIKOS" is a "household." It is made up of the people in our circle of influence. These are the people who share a common kinship, community, or interests with us.

The Gospel is universal, available for all to receive. In the same way, the way we *share* the Gospel is also universal.

THE TYPE "B" UNBELIEVER MAY HAVE ONE OF TWO PROBLEMS:

- **He or she does NOT know a Christian.**

  This is a problem of information. There's no one in this Oikos to share Christ.

- **He or she DOES know a Christian.**

  This is a problem of reputation. There's a Christian in this Oikos who is living a "double life."

- **Our task is to BUILD A BRIDGE of love to each life!**

THEY ARE AT DIFFERENT LEVELS, AND CANNOT BE TREATED IN THE SAME WAY.

There are 3 levels among "Type B" unbelievers:

- A large number of them are *unaware* that there is a significant difference between world religions and the personal, intimate relationship the Christian has with the Lord Jesus. *This group must hear the testimonies of Christians who know the difference.*

- Another group are *not receptive* because there are no people who love and serve them in Jesus' name. They can find no reason to spend time with Christians. *This group must be cultivated on a one-to-one basis.*

- The third group is open to *relationships* with Christians, but cannot find a common ground for developing them. *This is the group we will seek to bring to Christ through Share Groups.*

SERVING "TYPE B" UNBELIEVERS REQUIRES US TO BE AN "OIKONOMOS" WITHIN AN "OIKOS"

Luke 12:42: The Lord answered, "Who then is the faithful and wise manager, whom the master puts in charge of his servants to give them their food allowance at the proper time?"

The word used for "wise manager" is "OIKONOMOS." It refers to a person within the OIKOS who is given the task by the Master to provide the proper rations at the proper time to those in the OIKOS.

- PROPER RATIONS . . . at the
- PROPER TIME!

A baby doesn't eat the same food as an adult. So with Type "B" unbelievers. We must be sensitive to their needs and "eating habits" if we are to share the Gospel with them.

CONSIDER YOUR MINISTRY AT EACH LEVEL:

LEVEL 1:
The unbeliever is shown in detail how to become a Christian. In this series, you will learn to expand the presentation of John 3:16 to *The Master Plan.* It's more comprehensive, and covers the areas you'll need to share with "Type B" unbelievers.

LEVEL 2:
This unbeliever is now responsive to the study of the Bible. *The Way Home* New Testament has been prepared for you to use at this level.

LEVEL 3:
This is the level of Share Group life. Through continued contact with your team, the unbeliever recognizes your values are in contrast with his own. Life patterns are given serious thought. First you must establish a bond of friendship. Next, the Share Group team develops relationships with everyone.

LEVEL 4:

Many *distortions* about Christianity exist in the mind of the Level 4 unbeliever. These are the result of past experiences, creating *negative feelings or prejudices* implanted by family or friends. You must learn how to recognize these distortions, helping your friend to take a "new look" at our Lord.

LEVEL 5:

Frequently, the unbeliever at Level 5 will not know that becoming a Christian means you are "born again." With no knowledge of the facts about Christ's life, death, and resurrection, a person may assume that "living a good life" is the way to become a Christian. Your invasion of the OIKOS of an unbeliever is absolutely necessary!

Jesus Christ doesn't offer a set of laws, or a philosophy. He offers *HIMSELF* . . . and He dwells in you. At this level, your own sincere sharing of how you became a Christian is very, very important. It's just about the only way to help this unbeliever distinguish between a set of *beliefs* and having a very *personal relationship* with the Lord Jesus Christ.

LEVEL 1:
COMMITMENT

LEVEL 2:
BIBLE
STUDY
(The Way
Home N. T.)

LEVEL 3:
BODY
STUDY
(Share
Groups)

LEVEL 4: CREATE A RECEPTIVE ATTITUDE

LEVEL 5: SHARE YOUR TESTIMONY

SHARING HIS ANSWERS REGARDING EVERYTHING

"We loved you so much that we were delighted to share with you not only the gospel of God but our lives as well, because you had become so dear to us."
—1 Thessalonians 2:8

PROPER RATIONS FOR THE SHARE GROUP LEVEL

The purpose of a Share Group is to expose Type "B" unbelievers to relationships with Christians. Usually, these gatherings meet weekly, for 10 weeks, moving between the homes of all the members. As your Team meets with unbelievers, interest in the Gospel develops, later leading to in-depth Bible study using *"The Way Home"* NIV New Testament.

FACTS ABOUT SHARE GROUPS

- They provide an informal, non-threatening time where unbelievers can experience care and Christian truth.
- They provide an atmosphere of caring and trust, where people can truly be themselves without being rejected and condemned. Gradually, deep and abiding personal relationships develop.
- They provide a setting where individuals can work through their problems with the help and love of the others in the group. Solutions based on the scriptures are ultimately found.
- They provide a special structure for Team members to learn how their spiritual gifts work together in the ministry of evangelism.
- They enfold hurting ones in a blanket of prayer by intercessors. Unbelievers find others willing to minister to them.
- They last for ten weeks.
- "Body Life" is their method for sharing Christ's love.

- They meet at any time of the week. Each group sets its own schedule.
- The reason the group meets must be based on the *needs or interests of the unbelievers*, not on the needs of the Team members.
- Some Share Groups form for friendship. Others form to meet needs or hurts in the lives of the members. Still others are formed around a common interest.

SHARE GROUPS BUILD BRIDGES BETWEEN TEAM MEMBERS AND TYPE "B" UNBELIEVERS

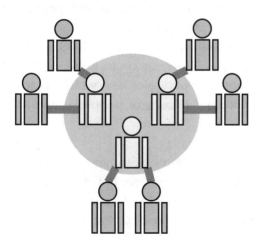

A Share Group with three Team members will include no more than six Type "B" unbelievers. There should always be a ratio of no more than two unbelievers for each Team member. Thus, the Share Group pictured has a total of nine persons, meeting together for 10 weeks.

Because group dynamics disintegrate if there are too many present, the absolute maximum for a Share Group Team would be four Team members. The ratio of two to one would then limit the largest Share Group to 12 persons.

Why is this important? Because, for this 10 week period, each Team member will seek to bond a close relationship with two of the group members. In addition to meeting weekly, there should be times when the Team member gets together with each Type "B" unbeliever. Personal attention must be shown. Confidences are shared. The unbeliever feels wanted and loved. *This is the heartbeat of a Share Group—forming a bond of love and concern between each Christian and unbeliever.* You can quickly realize that there isn't enough time in a week to carry on such friendships with more than two new people.

21

EACH TYPE "B" UNBELIEVER IS ALSO A BRIDGE INTO AN OIKOS OF PEOPLE

Your Share Group ministry will focus on building bridges with two Type "B" persons for 10 weeks. Then, the group completes its activity. You will not launch another group at this time. You will seek to cross over the bridge of your friendship into his or her OIKOS, and enlarge your ministry to those who have no contact with Christians.

As you do so, remember this fact:

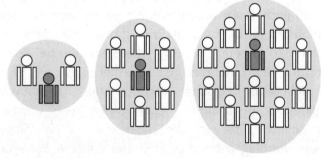

People who have been deeply hurt will have an OIKOS with only 3-5 people in it. Others, hurt less deeply, may include only 9 or 10. Thus, those who need Christ the

most have the *least contacts.* You, along with your fellow Team members, are the only bridge God now has to them. You create a bridge to them by your friendship. Then, you create a bridge between *them* and *the Lord Jesus* by sharing your faith.

EVERY PERSON OPENS UP A "WORLD" OF PEOPLE WHO LIVE IN HIS OR HER OIKOS

On page 8, you listed the names of 4 people you know who are not Christians. Two of them were Type "A" and two were Type "B." On the facing page, write the names of these four people. Then, list the names of people you know who are in their OIKOSES. How many of them do you know, or could know better? You are the beginning of a bridge of love which could bring the gospel to literally *dozens* of people as the months go by.

While not all people are searching for *Christ,* some of them are searching for *peace.* In Luke 10, Jesus said we are to penetrate OIKOSES (households) and offer our peace to *each one,* knowing that we may well find a true seeker!

YOUR "WORLD OF OIKOSES" DEMONSTRATED

At the top of each column, write the names of the four unbelievers from page 8. Beneath each name, write the names of people in their OIKOSES:

And Jesus came up and spoke to them, saying, "All authority has been given to Me in heaven and on earth. Go therefore and make disciples of all the nations, baptizing them in the name of the Father and the Son and the Holy Spirit, teaching them to observe all that I commanded you; and lo, I am with you always, even to the end of the age." ▪ Matthew 28:18-20

IF YOU WERE A TYPE "B" UNBELIEVER, WHY WOULD YOU WANT TO JOIN A SHARE GROUP?

Obviously, it would have to meet some need or cater to some interest you have in your life. *People don't commit to something they'e not interested in, do they?*

FACT: every Type "B" unbeliever listed on page 23 has a NEED or an INTEREST which is the bridge you can cross to create a relationship with him or her.

Let's see if that's true . . . return to page 23 and scan the list you have prepared. In the space to the right, transfer five of the names written there. Next to each name, indicate a NEED or an INTEREST which would cause that person to be responsive to your friendship:

NAME	INTEREST OR NEED

SMALL GROUP TIME: (10 MINUTES)

Discuss all the "Type B" people your Team members have listed on the previous page, and compare their NEEDS or INTERESTS.

Find one common NEED and one common INTEREST which appears on all your lists. Reorganize the names of the people accordingly, using the space to the right:

INTEREST

NAMES

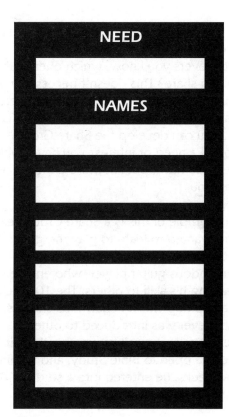

NEED

NAMES

25

NOW THAT YOU HAVE IDENTIFIED THE NEEDS AND INTERESTS OF THOSE IN YOUR OIKOSES, LET'S THINK ABOUT YOU . . .

Of the various needs and interests you have discovered to be among the Type "B" unbelievers you know, which ones of them do you share? This doesn't necessarily mean you are more of an "expert" in some area than they are. Sometimes the reverse is true . . . you can develop the Share Group around a need or interest *you* have, which they *also* have, but are more experienced than you.

An example of this is a Share Group Team who wanted to learn to play the guitar. One of the Team member's brothers was a tremendous guitar player, who enjoyed teaching his skill to others. The 10-week Share Group was an enormous success. This unbeliever was introduced to other musicians in the cell group church. He became open to Bible Study, and within a few weeks, he entered into a study of *The Way Home!*

WORKSHOP TIME

HOW WILL THIS WORK OUT FOR YOUR TEAM?
LET'S SEE . . .

1. As a team, list one or two INTERESTS which you have in common:

2. What NEEDS do you have in common?

3. Of your NEEDS and INTERESTS, which one might you focus on for your first Share Group experience?

4. List the names of at least six people in your OIKOS chains who would be interested in joining you in such a group:

27

HERE'S THE WAY TO SPEND THESE NEXT FEW WEEKS AS A SHARE GROUP TEAM:

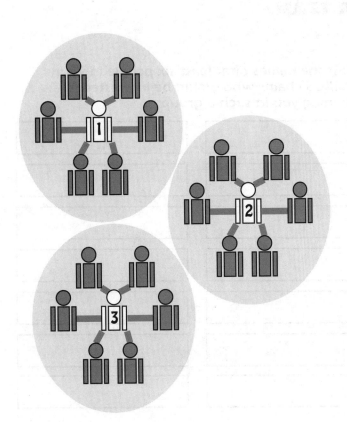

STEP ONE—THREE WEEKS: BUILD BRIDGES TO YOUR OWN CONTACTS

Simply being around the Type "B" people who may have an interest in your Share Group is the important first step. These persons probably are not related to you now on the level of being close friends, although you may have known each other for some time.

Ask yourself, *"How can I serve this person?"* We care about those who care about us! That's the way Jesus did His ministry, isn't it? It doesn't really matter *what* you do together, *as long as you're together!* Changing your lifestyle to have time for unbelievers is the greatest single hurdle you'll face. Shopping, talking, sharing in a recreation, eating out—be a part of the life of this person.

You will meet as a Team prior to each Cell Group meeting during the Equipping times. In this book, there are guidelines to help you report to each other on your progress. There's also a "Weekly Assignment" for you.

AFTER EACH OF YOU HAVE BONDED FRIENDSHIPS WITH TYPE "B" PERSONS, SHARE "GET-TOGETHERS" . . .

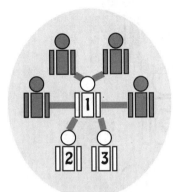

STEP TWO—THREE TO FIVE WEEKS:
BUILD BRIDGES TO YOUR TEAM MEMBERS

You may want to take three to five weeks for this second step. In the illustration, the first Share Group member has a "get-together" with Type "B" friends, and also invites the other two members of the Team. This is *not* presented as a group meeting. It may be a meal together, a party, or any activity appropriate for the lifestyles of the unbelievers.

The purpose of this event is to permit all three Share Group Team members to meet those who are being cultivated. Thus, each Team member conducts a "get-together" and invites his or her friends, plus the other two Team members.

It is not difficult to launch the Share Group once this "bridge" has been built. It's tough to agree to enter a 10-week commitment with people you don't know, isn't it? But, it's easy to do so if you have already met and enjoyed being with those who will be in the group with you.

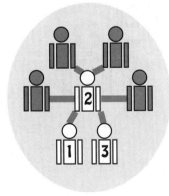

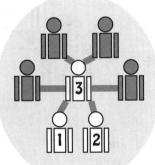

. . . THEN, LAUNCH YOUR SHARE GROUP!

STEP THREE:

When your Team members have entered the "comfort zones" of the Type "B" unbelievers, suggest you begin to meet together weekly. If you have selected a reason for the gathering that will *meet a need,* or *focus on an interest,* there will be an openness to their sharing in the activity.

At this time, each Team member should try to enlist *two persons* to be a part of the group. As you share together in the weeks ahead, there will be a spirit of belonging to each other which will continue for a long time to come.

The reason most people have so few friends is that they don't take the time to create them. While a small percentage of the population have an aversion to expanding their friendships, most are quite willing to do so *if they feel they will benefit as a result.*

God has anointed you to bring "Good News" to those who are hurting, lonely, oppressed, stepped on, and imprisoned. *Go into your ministry with the knowledge He abides in you—for them!*

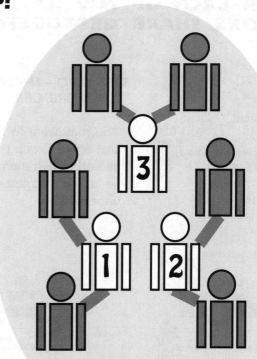

LET'S REVIEW THE MINISTRY ACTIVITIES FOR THE NEXT FEW WEEKS . . .

Place the dates for the next several weeks in this Countdown Calendar. It's a *guideline* to follow, but you may find your Team slightly revising it as the Lord opens hearts to you.

Note that for the next three weeks, each of you will be strengthening personal bonds between yourselves and your contacts. This period is followed by three weeks of "Get-Togethers." Finally, you invite those who are responsive to join the 10-week Share Group with your Team.

In the weeks that follow, you will be assisted by five daily Growth Guides to be covered each week. Don't do them all in one sitting! Space them so you do them Monday through Friday. They will mean the most to you if you meditate on each one for a day.

There are also guidelines for a WEEKLY ASSIGNMENT and your weekly TEAM MEETING in the pages which follow.

COUNTDOWN TO SHARE GROUP LAUNCH

WEEK 1: (Date)_____
Develop relationship with first Type "B" Unbeliever

WEEK 2: (Date)_____
Develop relationship with second Type "B" Unbeliever.

WEEK 3: (Date)_____
Develop relationship with third Type "B" Unbeliever.

WEEK 4: (Date)_____
Conduct first "Get-Together."

WEEK 5: (Date)_____
Conduct second "Get-Together."

WEEK 6: (Date)_____
Conduct third "Get-Together."

WEEK 7: (Date)_____
Each Team member invites two Type "B" Unbelievers to attend 10-week Share Group gatherings.

WEEK 8: (Date)_____
Team attends briefing for launching Share Group; Part 2, "Building Groups" manual is distributed.

WEEK 9: (Date)_____
Team shares in half night of prayer for their ministry.

WEEK 10: (Date)_____
SHARE GROUP LAUNCH

PRACTICAL ASSIGNMENT FOR WEEK ONE:

SPEND TIME WITH ONE OF YOUR OIKOS TYPE "B" PEOPLE

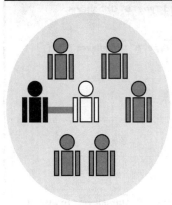

- PRAY! Ask the Lord to guide you as you choose the person you will spend time with this week.
- Schedule an activity with at LEAST one Type "B" unbeliever.
- Telephone each one of your Team members.
- Share the name of the person and the times you will be together.
- Ask the Team to hold you accountable for these times.

MY PLANS FOR THIS WEEK:

NAME OF PERSON I WILL SPEND TIME WITH THIS WEEK:

HOW WE WILL SPEND OUR TIME TOGETHER:

**IF WE SPEND OUR TIME ONE WAY, WE CAN'T ALSO SPEND IT ANOTHER WAY.
THE KEY TO REACHING PEOPLE FOR CHRIST IS TO SPEND TIME WITH THEM.
DURING THIS WEEK, RETHINK THE WAY YOU USE YOUR TIME.**

PRACTICAL ASSIGNMENT

REPORT TO TEAM MEMBERS

WRITE IN THIS SPACE THE REPORT OF THE
SHARING TIMES YOU HAD THIS WEEK
WITH TYPE "B" UNBELIEVERS

- Personal time:

- Telephone contacts:

WEEK 1, DAY 1
THIS WEEK: APPROACHING THE BRIDGE
TODAY: HOW DO YOU USE YOUR TIME?

Jot down the things you do each week...

	SUNDAY	MONDAY	TUESDAY	WEDNESDAY	THURSDAY	FRIDAY	SATURDAY
A.M.							
AFT.							
P.M.							

1. *READ PROVERBS 16:9.* What is the principle message it has for *you?*

2. Someone has said, *"We often spend our time accommodating impulses, rather than priorities."* What do you think this person meant by this?

_____

3. Which items below would you classify as "IMPULSE TIME?" *[Underline your answers]*

DAILY QUIET TIMES

PREPARING MEALS

WATCHING TV

AGREEING TO DO SOMETHING WHICH IS NOT IMPORTANT TO MY REAL PRIORITIES

ACCEPTING INVITATIONS TO DO THINGS, WHEN I REALLY NEED THAT TIME TO COMPLETE A RESPONSIBILITY

READING A MAGAZINE DURING TIME I SHOULD BE COMPLETING ASSIGNED WORK

4. List below four priorities you consider the highest in your life—in the order of their importance to you:

1._____

2._____

3._____

4._____

35

WEEK 1, DAY 2
THIS WEEK: APPROACHING THE BRIDGE
TODAY: IMPULSE TIME

"AM I CONTROLLED BY CIRCUMSTANCES?"

1. Yesterday, we observed the amount of time we waste by following IMPULSES. How much time could you "free up" to spend with Type "B" unbelievers each week if you simply use your IMPULSE TIME more wisely? Consider—among other things—the time you now use watching television:

_____

_____

(On the next lines, write how you really feel about this matter...)

_____

_____

2. Return to the last question you completed yesterday (Question 4). Did you list among the four most important things in your life *the sharing of Christ with Outsiders?* Probably not. Few Christians do! But—*why should it not be included as one of the most important activities of your life?*

3. *Read 1 Corinthians 7:29-31.* What does this passage suggest to you about the priorities Paul set for the use of his own time?

_____

_____

4. *Read John 4:40.* In your opinion, why did Jesus give a full two days of time to the Samaritans at Sychar (Remember that *all* of them were Outsiders!):

_____

_____

5. *Read Matthew 9:9-12.* Why do you think Jesus spent time eating with sinners?

_____

_____

6. Why is TIME the most important factor in reaching Type "B" unbelievers for Christ?

_____

_____

7. Return to the weekly calendar you completed yesterday: Look at the way you *now* spend your time. Can you see a way to release THREE HOURS EACH WEEK to use in ministering to Outsiders? How? *Or, why not?*

_____

_____

8. In *Tools for Time Management,* Ed Dayton says:

"The basic Christian priorities are first, commitment to God; second, commitment to the Body of Christ, His Church; third, commitment to the work of Christ."

Do you agree or disagree with his statement?

_____

_____

WEEK 1, DAY 3
THIS WEEK: APPROACHING THE BRIDGE
TODAY: "BUSYWORK"

1. Have you ever heard of "BUSYWORK?" Teachers give it to children when there are only a few minutes left before the end of the school day. "BUSYWORK" is activity which keeps little hands "busy." "BUSYWORK" also robs us of time to meet goals. Keeping busy with trivia can give us a false feeling of accomplishment. (An example of "BUSYWORK" is straightening up an entire room before sitting down to study. It's not helping to *learn* a thing!) Mark items in the list below which can become "BUSYWORK," not really leading to the goal of becoming a servant person. (You *will* find yourself arguing about your conclusions!)

   ☐ PLAYING GOLF   ☐ READING NOVELS

   ☐ SEWING   ☐ WATCHING TV

   ☐ TENNIS   ☐ GARDENING

   ☐ BOWLING

   ☐ COOKING GOURMET MEALS

   ☐ LISTENING TO SERMON TAPES

2. *Read Acts 20:24 and 1Corinthians 7:29-31.* What was Paul's attitude toward the use of time? What would he probably say to us about "BUSYWORK?"

   _____

   _____

3. Name three things Paul would probably call "BUSYWORK" (trivia) which Christians do today, thought by many to be an "important" part of life:

   1._____

   2._____

   3._____

4. A Christian spends 8 hours a week involved in church activities, but *not one of those hours* is spent in actual contact with Outsiders. Is this person correct in saying, "I already spend a lot of time serving the Lord; let *others* work with the unsaved!" Explain your answer:

_____

_____

5. Is it *possible* to spend time doing *"good things"* (like church work), and as a result miss doing the *right* things? If so, what should the Christian in the above situation do to spend adequate time with Outsiders?

_____

_____

_____

6. A man's goals were: (1) God first; (2) Christ's Body second; (3) Ministering to others third; (4) family fourth. He spent his time as follows:

WATCHING TV: 8 hours a week;

ATTENDING CHURCH: 4 hours a week;

PLAYING WITH CHILDREN: 3 hours a week;

FIXING UP HIS OLD CAR: 15 hours a week.

What advice would you give him?

_____

_____

_____

7. Are you a Christian who does "BUSYWORK" for the Lord—perhaps in the place of actually relating to unbelievers who need to know about Him?

☐ YES

☐ NO

WEEK 1, DAY 4
THIS WEEK: APPROACHING THE BRIDGE
TODAY: QUALITY TIME

1. *READ EPHESIANS 5:15-17.* Rewrite it in your own words:

_____

_____

2. What responsibility do we have to put our use of time under the Lordship of Jesus Christ?

_____

_____

3. *Read Colossians 4:5-6.* what does it mean to "make the most of the opportunity?"

_____

4. Being *with* a Type "B" unbeliever is not enough. QUALITY TIME means that you are willing to really *concentrate* on what is being said, seeking to understand the deepest needs of the person. To have QUALITY TIME, you must be certain there's adequate time to share deeply with one another. Interruptions can *ruin* such times. The PLACE, therefore, is very important when spending QUALITY TIME with unbelievers.

Use yourself as an example. A *stranger* meets you: How much time would that person have to spend with you before you would ...
(WRITE THE ESTIMATED TIME IN THE BLANKS)

_____FEEL AT EASE WITH THIS STRANGER

_____WILLINGLY DISCUSS PERSONAL NEEDS

_____SHARE YOUR DEEPEST WORRIES

5. What can you conclude from the above question? How important do you feel it is to find QUALITY TIME to give to Outsiders, if they are to be won to Christ?

_____

_____

6. A Christian spent fifteen minutes getting acquainted with his new neighbor. He then proceeded to share his faith in Christ, encouraging the neighbor to also become a Christian. Ever since then, his neighbor has avoided him. CAN YOU LIST THREE REASONS WHY?

   1._____

   2._____

   3._____

7. What would be a better way to approach the same situation?

_____

_____

WEEK 1, DAY 5
THIS WEEK: APPROACHING THE BRIDGE
TODAY: PRIORITIZING YOUR TIME

READ LUKE 19:10. From this verse, why do you think Jesus spent so much time with Outsiders?

_____

_____

_____

_____

At this time in your training, you are asked to face a commitment to *deliberately set aside approximately 3 hours a week to minister (to serve)* Type "B" unbelievers. It is not possible for you to effectively reach unbelievers unless you are willing to give them *TIME!* Count the cost—*not of your time,* but of the *lives* which will spend eternity apart from Christ if you do NOT restructure your lifestyle to find time for them!

PRAY EARNESTLY ABOUT THIS MATTER
BEFORE PROCEEDING...

Ask the Father to guide your heart and your hand as you fill out the following Weekly Calendar. In doing so, let it be a Covenant between yourself and your Lord: from this time onward, be prepared to give Type "B" unbelievers up to three hours a week!

	SUNDAY	MONDAY	TUESDAY	WEDNESDAY	THURSDAY	FRIDAY	SATURDAY
9							
10							
11							
12							
1							
2							
3							
4							
5							
6							
7							
8							
9							

COUNTDOWN TO SHARE GROUP LAUNCH

WEEK 1: (Date)_____
Develop relationship with first Type "B" Unbeliever

WEEK 2: (Date)_____
Develop relationship with second Type "B" Unbeliever.

WEEK 3: (Date)_____
Develop relationship with third Type "B" Unbeliever.

WEEK 4: (Date)_____
Conduct first "Get-Together."

WEEK 5: (Date)_____
Conduct second "Get-Together."

WEEK 6: (Date)_____
Conduct third "Get-Together."

WEEK 7: (Date)_____
Each Team member invites two Type "B" Unbelievers to attend 10-week Share Group gatherings.

WEEK 8: (Date)_____
Team attends briefing for launching Share Group; Part 2, "Building Groups" manual is distributed.

WEEK 9: (Date)_____
Team shares in half night of prayer for their ministry.

WEEK 10: (Date)_____
SHARE GROUP LAUNCH

WEEK ONE
CELL GROUP EQUIPPING TIME

THE TEAM SHARES...

UP TO 3 MINUTES PER PERSON:

- **Team members share reports on working with "Type B" Unbelievers**
- **Share other items you noted on your REPORT SHEET (page33) with the Team.**

- **SCHEDULE THE THREE "GET-TOGETHERS" YOU WILL CONDUCT DURING WEEKS 5, 6, AND 7:**

  Week 5:

  Date:_____ **Time:**_____ **Place:**_____

  Week 6:

  Date:_____ **Time:**_____ **Place:**_____

  Week 7:

  Date:_____ **Time:**_____ **Place:**_____

- **(As time permits:) COMPARE YOUR THOUGHTS ABOUT HOW YOUR TIME HAS BEEN ABUSED IN THE PAST.**

PRACTICAL ASSIGNMENT FOR WEEK TWO:

SPEND TIME WITH ANOTHER TYPE "B" UNBELIEVER

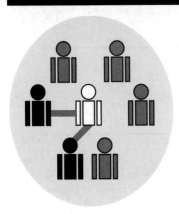

- PRAY! Ask the Lord to guide you as you choose the next person you will spend time with this week.
- Schedule an activity with ANOTHER Type "B" Unbeliever.
- Keep in touch with the person you shared with last week.
- Telephone each one of your Team members.
- Share the name of the person and the times you will be together this week.

MY PLANS FOR THIS WEEK:

NAME OF PERSON I WILL SPEND TIME WITH THIS WEEK:

HOW WE WILL SPEND OUR TIME TOGETHER:

YOU CAN GIVE WITHOUT LOVING, BUT YOU CAN'T LOVE WITHOUT GIVING.
GOD GAVE HIS SON BECAUSE HE WAS HIS MOST PRECIOUS TREASURE.
GIVING YOURSELF AND YOUR TIME TO AN UNBELIEVER IS A PRECIOUS TREASURE, TOO!

WRITE IN THIS SPACE THE REPORT OF THE
SHARING TIMES YOU HAD THIS WEEK
WITH TYPE "B" UNBELIEVERS

- Personal time:

- Telephone contacts:

WEEK 2, DAY 1
THIS WEEK: CROSSING THE BRIDGE—HOW TO CONDUCT YOURSELF
TODAY: HAVE A POSITIVE VIEW OF EACH PERSON

1. *Read Luke 19:1-10.*
   Zacchaeus was hated by the Jews. He was a cheat, a merciless tax man, and thought only of himself. In verse 5, where did Jesus want to meet this man? (Underline your answer:)

   In the Synagogue

   In his *oikos (house)*

   In secret, where no one would know about it

2. Verse 7 says *"they"* all began to "grumble among themselves..." In your opinion, how many of the people residing in Jericho disliked Zacchaeus? (Underline your answer)

   Only the Pharisees.

   Only those Zacchaeus had unfairly taxed.

   Everyone in the town.

3. Jesus saw something in the man Zacchaeus that others could not see. Read verses 3, 4, and 6: what did Jesus discern in him that others did not? (Write your own words and conclusions:)

   _____

   _____

   _____

4. What is *your* natural reaction to people who take advantage of you and others, who—without conscience—use situations for their selfish purposes?

   _____

   _____

   _____

48

5. Can you think of a "Type B" Unbeliever you know who might be *your* Zacchaeus? Don't write his/her name down, but *think about this person . . .*

6. Meditate on this thought: *if Jesus had taken the same attitude toward Zacchaeus as everyone else, what would have been his destiny?*

_____

_____

_____

7. Why do you think Jesus entered this man's *oikos?*

_____

_____

8. Rewrite, in your own words, verse 10:

_____

_____

_____

A TRUE STORY . . .

As I travelled across America preaching and teaching, I met a number of Christian physicians who had been won to Christ while they were studying at Baylor College of Medicine in Houston, Texas. All of them had made their decision through the influence of one woman, who conducted a student ministry there.

Several years later, I met this legendary lady at a dinner party. I drew her aside and asked, "You have left a trail of conversions behind you! Many of the doctors told me they were cynical, sarcastic atheists when they met you. *What was the secret of your influence for Christ in their lives?*

She responded, "There's no secret. All I did was believe in them when they didn't believe in themselves. I saw them not as they were, *but as they would be when Jesus came to live in their lives."*

You will bless many Type "B" Unbelievers if you will see them through the eyes of Jesus! Let this truth saturate your thoughts as you relate to your unconverted contacts this week.

—Ralph W. Neighbour, Jr.

WEEK 2, DAY 2
THIS WEEK: CROSSING THE BRIDGE—HOW TO CONDUCT YOURSELF
TODAY: LEARN TO LISTEN, PART 1

Read Proverbs 1:5

There are four types of communication. In the list below, rate the four types according to the *formal training* you have received for each one (1=Most; 4=Least):

_____READING

_____WRITING

_____SPEAKING

_____LISTENING

Most people rate LISTENING as "Least." We are taught for years to read and write during our school years, While many of us have taken a course in public speaking, our parents taught us how to talk from our earliest childhood.

However, few of us have been trained to listen!

If we never learn how to listen, we will never really, deeply understand another human being from that person's frame of reference. If you want to bring the love of Christ and relate effectively to a Type "B" Unbeliever, you must first understand this person.

The real key to your influence with an unbeliever is your example, your actual conduct. Your example flows naturally out of your character, or the kind of person you truly are—not what you want others to *think* you are. If your character is constantly radiating, others will instinctively trust you.

If your life reveals moments of kindness and moments of brittleness, the unbeliever will not feel safe enough to expose opinions and tender feelings. Even though a lost person needs the Christ you offer, your advice may not be accepted. Therefore, you must build the skills of listening that inspire trust and openness.

SEEK FIRST TO UNDERSTAND, NOT TO BE UNDERSTOOD

Usually, we focus on being understood. Instead, we must learn to get inside another person's way of seeing the world. Once you do this, you see the world the way they see the world, and you understand how they feel.

It's easy to transfer our beliefs and values into another person, *distorting* what that individual knows and values. To serve others, we must guard against the tendency to assume our beliefs make sense to them. To do this effectively, we must learn to *listen carefully* to what is being said.

WEEK 2, DAY 3
THIS WEEK: CROSSING THE BRIDGE—HOW TO CONDUCT YOURSELF
TODAY: LEARN TO LISTEN, PART 2

Read 1 Corinthians 2:14-15

When a Type "B" Unbeliever speaks, we often listen at one of four levels:

- IGNORING
  ("What am I going to say next?")
- PRETENDING
  ("Yes. Uh-huh. Right . . .")
- SELECTIVE LISTENING
  (We choose the portions we want to hear . . .)
- ATTENTIVE LISTENING
  (Paying attention to what is being said . . .)

However, there's another level of listening. At this fifth level, we seek to *understand* the needs, the fears, the joys, and the strong convictions of the other person. This sort of listening is powerful because it gives you an understanding of spiritual needs and awarenesses.

Instead of assuming thoughts and feelings, you're dealing with the reality inside another person's head and heart. *You are listening to understand!*

Remember this important fact: *satisfied needs do not open a person to Jesus Christ.* Only the unsatisfied needs do that. After physical survival, the greatest need of a human being is to be understood and to be appreciated. When you *really listen,* you are going to be welcomed into the depths of another person's life.

Sin is like a bee sting. It leaves a sore spot. When you find that sting, you have discovered the reason that person will want to know about The Great Healer.

Jesus said he would bring good news to the poor, the broken hearted, the imprisoned, and to the blind. Which need exists in the hearts of the Type "B" Unbelievers you are seeking to win to Christ?

DIAGNOSE BEFORE YOU PRESCRIBE!

If your unbelieving friend doesn't feel you truly understand the situations within his or her life, your recommendation for the "cure" will be doubted. Seeking first to understand is a very important principle in all areas of life—and it's even more so in seeking to bond a friendship with an unbeliever. Here are some diagnostic questions:

HOW DOES THIS PERSON VIEW CHRISTIANITY?

*   Extent of previous exposure:

    _____

*   Clearness of understanding:

    _____

*   Attitudes caused by family tradition:

    _____

*   Attitudes caused by previous contact with Christians:

    _____

WHAT ARE THE FOCAL POINTS OF THIS PERSON?

*   Personal needs:

    _____

*   Personal values:

    _____

*   Overriding ambitions:

    _____

*   Way the meaning of life is interpreted:

    _____

HOW DOES THIS PERSON "SEE" JESUS CHRIST?

*   What true facts about Jesus are known?

    _____

*   Where were they learned?

    _____

WEEK 2, DAY 4
THIS WEEK: CROSSING THE BRIDGE—HOW TO CONDUCT YOURSELF
TODAY: BE AWARE OF BODY LANGUAGE

As you visit with Type "B" Unbelievers, learn to read "body language." If you are sensitive to it, you will be able to discern when you are accepted, when you are boring your friend, and when you are being too threatening with your remarks.

For example, *the eyes* are the most expressive part of a human body. Facial expressions, body posture, open or clenched hands, also "say" things.

Folded arms communicate uneasiness or defensiveness. If a person covers the face with both hands or one hand, it may be communicating shame or withdrawal.

In the illustration to the right, the posture of the person obviously denotes boredom. *What are the signs which reveal this?*

A MOST IMPORTANT "BODY LANGUAGE" SIGNAL RELATES TO SPIRITUAL RESPONSES

Heart-hunger for God is frequently communicated first in a non-verbal way. Watch for the wistful look of longing in the eye, the leaning forward on the chair to listen more attentively, the nod of the head which agrees and says, "I'm like that!"

Other non-verbal signals may communicate *rejection* of what you are talking about. These may include:

- A look of hardness; "steel in the eyes."
- Nervousness when Christ's name is mentioned

"Body Language" also reveals *emotional* responses. For example, *anxiety* is revealed by profuse sweating. *Depression* is revealed by tears which flow too quickly and too freely. *Anger* or *fear* is revealed by a flushed skin color.

Such signals don't require a trained eye—only a sympathetic one! Don't miss such signals.

Gradually, you will learn to catch non-verbal clues that the Type "B" Unbeliever is searching for something. The little cough, or clearing of the throat, reveals insecurity or embarrassment. The downcast eyes signals to you that it may be the right time to ask, "Is there something that we need to share about? —Something that you are thinking about right now?"

LEARN NOW TO BE SENSITIVE TO THE "BODY LANGUAGE" OF YOUR UNBELIEVING FRIENDS!

As you begin to meet together in small groups, you should have developed a sensitivity to all the non-verbal signals used by people. Who is sitting on the edge of the chair? Who is slumped back, in a gesture of withdrawal? Who has folded arms, denoting a posture of self-protection? Who is "poker-faced?"

OH, YES . . .

Before we leave this subject, remember your own "Body Language" is constantly speaking—even when you are silent. Avoid certain gestures which "talk" when you are listening. For example, if you put your finger tips together, with your hands on the arms of your chair, you are "steepling." It infers you feel superior to the person engaged in conversation.

THIS WEEK: CROSSING THE BRIDGE—HOW TO CONDUCT YOURSELF
TODAY: SELF-DISCLOSURE TAKES COURAGE

HOW MUCH OF YOURSELF
DO YOU EXPOSE TO OTHERS?

In the illustration on the opposite page, note the way the people are hiding their true faces from one another, masking their true feelings. Have you ever been with people who do that?

Satan has created a world in which men seek to accommodate others. People often act to please others, even when they compromise to do so. When Christians do this, they may deliberately hide their true identity!

Read Matthew 26:69-74.

1. In the scripture above, what were the motives you feel caused Peter to deny his identity with Christ? *(Underline your answers:)*

   Fear of being arrested

   Denied Jesus because he didn't like Him

   Wished to be liked by the people around him

   Disillusioned because Jesus stopped him when he cut off the soldier's ear

2. When you have spent time with unbelievers in the past, has there been a tendency to hide your witness and your identity as a Christian? *If so, how can your Team provide support for you as you minister now?*

WAYS MY TEAM CAN SUPPORT ME:

_____

_____

_____

Ministering along with your Team members will make sharing your faith with Type "B" Unbelievers easier than doing it by yourself. That's one of the reasons why Jesus always sent His disciples two by two, and why Paul was always accompanied by one or more companions.

As you make contacts with unbelievers this week, plan to introduce them to Team members quickly. That's one of the reasons for the "Get-Togethers" you will be holding soon!

And—when you are alone with unbelievers—*remember who your Master is!*

COUNTDOWN TO SHARE GROUP LAUNCH

WEEK 1: (Date)_____
Develop relationship with first Type "B" Unbeliever

WEEK 2: (Date)_____
Develop relationship with second Type "B" Unbeliever.

WEEK 3: (Date)_____
Develop relationship with third Type "B" Unbeliever.

WEEK 4: (Date)_____
Conduct first "Get-Together."

WEEK 5: (Date)_____
Conduct second "Get-Together."

WEEK 6: (Date)_____
Conduct third "Get-Together."

WEEK 7: (Date)_____
Each Team member invites two Type "B" Unbelievers to attend 10-week Share Group gatherings.

WEEK 8: (Date)_____
Team attends briefing for launching Share Group; Part 2, "Building Groups" manual is distributed.

WEEK 9: (Date)_____
Team shares in half night of prayer for their ministry.

WEEK 10: (Date)_____
SHARE GROUP LAUNCH

WEEK TWO
CELL GROUP EQUIPPING TIME

THE TEAM SHARES...

UP TO 3 MINUTES PER PERSON:

- **Team members share reports on responses of "Type B" Unbelievers contacted**
- **Share other items you noted on your REPORT SHEET (page 47) with the Team.**

USE THIS PAGE TO PLAN THE "GET-TOGETHER" YOU WILL CONDUCT DURING WEEK 4:

Date:_____ **Time:**_____ **Place:**_____

ACTIVITY	ASSIGNED TO:	REMARKS

PRACTICAL ASSIGNMENT FOR WEEK THREE:

1. SPEND TIME WITH ANOTHER TYPE "B" PERSON

- PRAY! Ask the Lord to guide you as you choose the next person you will spend time with this week.
- Schedule an activity with ANOTHER Type "B" Unbeliever.
- Keep in touch with the persons you shared with in past weeks.
- Telephone each one of your Team members.
- Share the name of the persons and the times you will be with them this week.

2. INVITE UNBELIEVERS TO ATTEND YOUR "GET-TOGETHER."

DATE FOR MY "GET-TOGETHER:" _____

NAMES OF THOSE INVITED	CONFIRMED

WRITE IN THIS SPACE THE REPORT OF THE SHARING TIMES YOU HAD THIS WEEK WITH TYPE "B" UNBELIEVERS

- Personal time:

- Telephone contacts:

- Names of those who have confirmed they will come to my "Get-Together"

WEEK 3, DAY 1
THIS WEEK: OVER THE BRIDGE—THINGS TO REMEMBER
TODAY: PHYSICAL SETTINGS ARE IMPORTANT

PHYSICAL SETTINGS
DRASTICALLY INFLUENCE GROUPS!

As you plan for the three "Get-Togethers," you and your Team should give some thought to the impact of their *physical settings.* Here are some pointers to remember:

1. Telephone calls can be disruptive. Can someone in the family be assigned to answer them? Or, better yet, can the phone be disconnected?

2. Pets that run in and out at will can be a problem. Some people don't enjoy animals.. Can the pet be put in a room with the door closed?

3. Children who run through the room, crying for a parent, etc., can ruin a "Get-Together." Can someone care for them in another area? Or, can you make arrangements for a joint baby sitter, perhaps keeping the children at a nearby residence?

4. Non-participating family members who play their music at full volume, or who watch television nearby, can keep a group from being effective.

5. Almost always, it's wise to provide refreshments at the BEGINNING of the "Get-Together." People come slowly to a gathering, and the waiting time for the last one to arrive can be spent drinking coffee or munching. If the group will meet around a table, a dish of snacks may be placed in the center of it.

**IF YOU ARE HOSTING A GROUP,
BE SENSITIVE TO THESE DETAILS!**

CHAIR ARRANGEMENT

A good host or hostess will recognize that the physical setting of the room can make or destroy a feeling of "togetherness."

In the original position, the furniture in this illustration divides people into 4 zones:

- The Couch

- The Pair Of Chairs

- Two Chairs, unrelated to any cluster

It is very hard to have a good group meeting in this setting. It would be better to move the chairs as indicated. This would provide a warm, intimate setting. A coffee table in the center of the new circle would be a good idea.

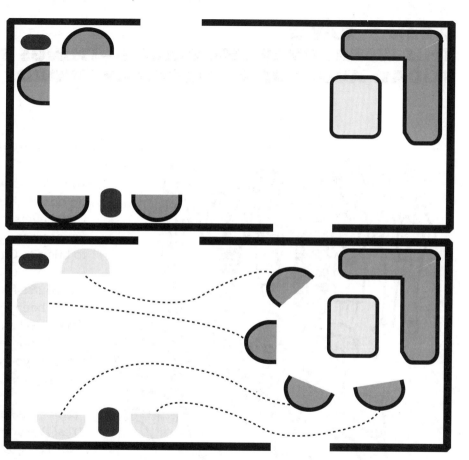

WEEK 3, DAY 2
THIS WEEK: OVER THE BRIDGE—THINGS TO REMEMBER
TODAY: AVOID USING "CHURCHY" WORDS

Read 1 Corinthians 9:19-23

Those of us who are believers must be careful that we do not act like we are the "insiders," and that Type "B" Unbelievers are "outsiders." In doing so, we create an unnecessary gap between ourselves and those we wish to bring to Christ.

Put yourself in the place of an unbeliever. Perhaps you have been cultivating this person, and you have developed a real bond of friendship. You then introduce one of your fellow Team members to him or her. As the three of you are visiting together, your Team member says to you:

"Didn't we have a great time at church camp?"
"Yes! Are you going to the first service this Sunday?"
"No, I'm going to the second one. Wasn't that a great sermon Pastor preached last week?"

WHEN YOU ARE WITH UNBELIEVERS, TALK ABOUT THINGS WHICH INCLUDE THEM!

How do you think Type "B" Unbelievers react to such conversations?

Thoughts like these may be their reaction:

"What's going on here? I thought the three of us were going to visit with each other. I have nothing to say now. I didn't go to that church camp, I don't plan to go to their church this Sunday, and I didn't hear the sermon they are raving about. I feel uncomfortable. I think I'll find an excuse to cut this short and leave them."

When we engage in "insider talk," unbelievers feel that a plate glass window has been slammed down, separating them from us. Regrettably, Christians who talk this way are usually insensitive to what they are doing to damage a relationship. It's the result of living in isolation from people who are not in "our world." We have allowed our own activities to become the center of our attention, unaware that others do not share our lifestyles or our values.

In 1 Corinthians 9:19-23, Paul said he "became like a Jew...like one under the law...like one not under the law...like one having the law...like one who was weak..."

Can you explain why he made these statements, as noted in verse 22-23?

_____

_____

_____

_____

Think about this! You must become what *unbelievers* need you to be for them. It's really an act of selfishness to exclude them with such "church talk," isn't it?

DOES THIS MEAN WE MUST NEVER SHARE OUR LIFE IN CHRIST?

Of course not! Bringing a report of your life in Christ, and your activities as a Christian, is always appropriate. *Just don't do it in a way that excludes the unbeliever!*

WEEK 3, DAY 3
THIS WEEK: OVER THE BRIDGE—THINGS TO REMEMBER
TODAY: DON'T ASSUME EVERYONE BELIEVES WHAT YOU BELIEVE

Read Matthew 16:13-14

When ministering to Type "B" Unbelievers, it's easy to think that they believe the same things you believe. It's usually a mistake to do that. For example, look at this illustration—*what do you see?*

"FRAME OF REFERENCE" REFERS TO THE WAY EACH PERSON SEES AND INTERPRETS HIS WORLD

This is called a "Frame of Reference" test. Some people see two faces. Others see a goblet. The picture itself "looks" the same to all—*but people see different things in it.* The differences are called the person's "Frame of Reference."

Each person develops a special reference to spiritual truths. This takes place over a long period of time. It is influenced by many factors.

66

OIKOS PROFILE SHEET

NAME _____ AGE _____ PHONE _____

STREET _____ CITY _____ ZIP _____

RESPONSE LEVEL

☐ Hardened to the gospel, bitter toward religion, antagonistic

☐ Open, but no depth in spiritual matters

☐ Interested, but preoccupied with things of the world

☐ A "Man of Peace," searching, open, responsive

CONTACT POINT

What are his/her felt needs? _____

What are his/her likes and interests? _____

Does he/she have a "hole in the heart" (A deep pain that has not healed)? _____

Has there been a recent crisis? _____

Is there an approaching special event, such as marriage or graduation, birth of a baby, loss of a job, etc.? _____

What are the prayer needs in this person's life? _____

PERSONAL MINISTRY

Who can best minister and love this person into an Oikos relationship? _____

How can a Christian become part of this Oikos? _____

Is there a way to develop a deeper personal relationship? _____

How can the Cell minister in love to this person? _____

GROUP EXPERIENCE

What type of Cultivation Group does this person need?

☐ A ministry group for specific needs, such as alcoholism, battered wives, etc.

☐ A target group for felt needs, such as loneliness or stress

☐ A Share Group for neutral or questioning persons—leading to a philosophical discussion of scripture, leading to openness

☐ A group for the open and interested, using "The Way Home" New Testament with "Handbook for Successful Living," leading to a point of decision to accept Christ.

REMEMBER—WHEN GOD OPENS A HEART, A LEVEL 5, 4, 3, OR 2 PERSON SHOULD BE INVITED TO ACCEPT JESUS CHRIST! DON'T EVER DELAY OFFERING SALVATION TO THOSE WHO ARE RESPONSIVE. LET THE HOLY SPIRIT GUIDE YOU!

"GET-TOGETHER" REPORT SHEET

COMPLETE ONE OF THESE SHEETS FOR EACH "GET-TOGETHER" YOUR TEAM CONDUCTS. TURN IT IN TO YOUR CELL LEADER.

THIS REPORT WILL BE PRAYERFULLY EVALUATED BY LEADERSHIP TO LEARN FROM YOUR EXPERIENCE

SHARE EVERYTHING THAT MIGHT HELP OTHERS IN THE FUTURE!

CELL GROUP: _____   DATE OF "GET TOGETHER" _____

NAMES OF TEAM MEMBERS:

(CHECK THE NAME OF THE TEAM MEMBER WHO HOSTED THE GATHERING)

☐ _____   LOCATION: _____

☐ _____

☐ _____

ACTIVITIES REPORT

List the NAMES and ADDRESSES of those who attended as guests of the Team Member:

Names: Addresses:

_____   _____

_____   _____

_____   _____

Describe the "Get-Together:"

1. Briefly outline the event, from the first thing you did to the last thing:

_____

_____

_____

2. What did you learn about the guests as you went through the QUAKER QUESTIONS?

_____

_____

_____

3. What will you do differently next time?

_____

_____

4. What would you like to pass on to other Teams from your experience?

_____

_____

REVIEW CARD (PUT IN YOUR BIBLE)

I have shared the following verses with fellow Team members, and they have affirmed I have memorized them:

SCRIPTURE VERSE

VERIFIED BY TEAM MEMBER
(Signature Or Initials)

WEEK 1: GENESIS 3:5

WEEK 2: ROMANS 2:5

WEEK 3: ISAIAH 64:6

WEEK 4: LUKE 19:10

WEEK 5: 1 PETER 2:24

WEEK 6: ROMANS 10:9

WEEK 7: 1 JOHN 1:9

WEEK 8: 2 CORINTHIANS 6:2

WEEK 7
Hope For Sinning Christians

If we confess our sins, He is faithful and righteous to forgive us our sins and to cleanse us from all unrighteousness.

1 JOHN 1:9

WEEK 5
The Cross Of Jesus

And He Himself bore our sins in His body on the cross, that we might die to sin and live to righteousness; for by His wounds you were healed.

1 PETER 2:24

WEEK 3
Righteousness Like Filthy Rags

For all of us have become like one who is unclean, And all our righteous deeds are like a filthy garment; And all of us wither like a leaf, And our iniquities, like the wind, take us away.

ISAIAH 64:6

WEEK 1
The Desire To Be Like God

"For God knows that in the day you eat from it your eyes will be opened, and you will be like God, knowing good and evil."

GENESIS 3:5

WEEK 8
Do It Now!

For He says, "At the acceptable time I listened to you, and on the day of salvation I helped you"; behold, now is "The acceptable time," behold, now is "The day of Salvation"—

2 CORINTHIANS 6:2

WEEK 6
How Salvation Comes

That if you confess with your mouth Jesus as Lord, and believe in your heart that God raised Him from the dead, you shall be saved.

ROMANS 10:9

WEEK 4
Hope For The Lost

"For the Son of Man has come to seek and to save that which was lost."

LUKE 19:10

WEEK 2
Storing Up Wrath

But because of your stubbornness and unrepentant heart you are storing up wrath for yourself in the day of wrath and revelation of the righteous judgment of God.

ROMANS 2:5

INSTRUCTIONS FOR MEMORIZING

SCRIPTURES FOR USE WITH TYPE "B" UNBELIEVERS

1. Cut out the cards.
2. Memorize one verse each week for eight weeks.
3. Carry the cards with you. Use odd moments (travel time, for example) to memorize.
4. Review verses already learned by using the reference side of the card.
5. Repeat the reference before and after you recite the verse. This will help you remember where it is found in your Bible.
6. Recite the verses to fellow Team members when you have your weekly Team Meeting.
7. Pray for openings to use these scriptures. In the next module, you will learn how to use them with a diagram.

WEEK 7
Hope For Sinning Christians

1 JOHN 1:9

WEEK 8
Do It Now!

2 Corinthians 6:2

WEEK 5
The Cross Of Jesus

1 PETER 2:24

WEEK 6
How Salvation Comes

ROMANS 10:9

WEEK 3
Righteousness Like Filthy Rags

ISAIAH 64:6

WEEK 4
Hope For The Lost

LUKE 19:10

WEEK 1
The Desire To Be Like God

GENESIS 3:5

WEEK 2
Storing Up Wrath

ROMANS 2:5

STUDY THE FIGURE BELOW:
HOW MANY SQUARES DO YOU SEE?

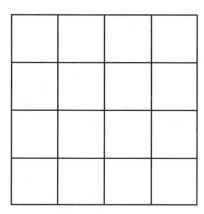

Most people see sixteen.
Some people, however, see more.
A few will discover there are a total of 30 squares.

Nearly all can eventually "see" all of the squares, but not until an explanation has been patiently given.

You see, all of us "see" things from our own perspective. Therefore, it's important to discern what the Type "B" Unbeliever accepts about Jesus Christ, and where this information was gleaned..

IN THINKING OF HOW THE GOSPEL MAY BE SEEN BY AN UNBELIEVER, THESE FACTORS MUST BE CONSIDERED:

1. When, and where, did this person learn something about the Christian message?

2. What half-truths were taught?

3. What truths were not taught at all?

4. What Christians (if any) has this person known?

5. How effectively has the Christian life been "modelled" for this person?

6. What have family beliefs and loyalties to religion done to shape wł   is known?

7. What hurts from the past are related to the Christian message?

As you relate to those you are praying for and working with, seek to understand these matters. Don't assume that when you say "God" they are defining the word as you are doing. They probably are not!

67

WEEK 3, DAY 4
THIS WEEK: OVER THE BRIDGE—THINGS TO REMEMBER
TODAY: UNDERSTANDING THE CONCERNS OF THE UNBELIEVER

Read Matthew 6:31-32

According to this passage, what three things do "pagans" run after?

1. _____

2. _____

3. _____

Let's contrast those three things with the things *you* "run after:"

1. _____

2. _____

3. _____

Satan's great task is to preoccupy his subjects with concerns which will blind them to spiritual matters. His inventory of concerns is endless!

Consider the ways people preoccupy themselves. Here is a person concerned about cars, and there is one who is occupied with decorating a home. Still another focuses on sports, or collecting wealth, or building a business.

That powerful, dominating obsession is the *primary stronghold* in the life of each person. Because of it, each one lives in a spiritual prison cell. Jesus told us such persons are deaf and blind to the things of the Spirit.

Your prayer life is the tool to unlock such prisons. As you take these blinding concerns before the Lord and intercede for them, God will work in a new way to set these captives free!

In the weeks you have been relating to your unbelieving friends, have you discovered the *primary concern* held by each one? Llist them in the space below:

Name: _____

    Primary Concern: _____

Name: _____

    Primary Concern: _____

Name: _____

    Primary Concern: _____

Jesus went to great lengths to teach that our greatest activity is to be *the servant of all.* As you understand the primary concern of the Type "B" Unbeliever, ask yourself, *"How can I serve this person?"*

A TRUE STORY . . .

When I was a child, my Dad made friends with the father of one of my best friends, Jimmy Crumley. Mr. Crumley was a Type "B" Unbeliever, and had no time for God in his lifestyle. His Primary Concern was not his family or his work. *It was Amateur Radio.* He had a massive antenna system in a field next to his house, and would spend hours nightly talking to other amateurs all over the world. His family seldom talked to him, but men in Asia and Europe, Africa and South America, knew him well.

My Dad developed a deep burden for Mr. Crumley, who had no interest in striking up a friendship. After much prayer, the Lord showed Dad that he had to become involved in Mr. Crumley's obsession. Meekly, he asked him, "Would you teach me about Amateur Radio?"

For many weeks, I fell asleep to the clicking sounds of my Dad learning the Morse Code in the next room. He invested hours learning to "fit" into Mr. Crumley's life. Several months later, Jimmy and I watched with joy as this man confessed Christ as Lord. It was one of my first examples of a man winning another by paying the price to enter his Primary Concern at a great sacrifice of time. Oh, by the way—Mr. Crumley became a deeply committed Christian!

—Ralph W. Neighbour, Jr.

COUNTDOWN TO SHARE GROUP LAUNCH

WEEK 1: (Date)_____
Develop relationship with first Type "B" Unbeliever

WEEK 2: (Date)_____
Develop relationship with second Type "B" Unbeliever.

WEEK 3: (Date)_____
Develop relationship with third Type "B" Unbeliever.

WEEK 4: (Date)_____
Conduct first "Get-Together."

WEEK 5: (Date)_____
Conduct second "Get-Together."

WEEK 6: (Date)_____
Conduct third "Get-Together."

WEEK 7: (Date)_____
Each Team member invites two Type "B" Unbelievers to attend 10-week Share Group gatherings.

WEEK 8: (Date)_____
Team attends briefing for launching Share Group; Part 2, "Building Groups" manual is distributed.

WEEK 9: (Date)_____
Team shares in half night of prayer for their ministry.

WEEK 10: (Date)_____
SHARE GROUP LAUNCH

WEEK THREE
CELL GROUP EQUIPPING TIME

THE TEAM SHARES...

UP TO 3 MINUTES PER PERSON:

- **Team members share reports on working with "Type B" Unbelievers**
- **Share other items you noted on your REPORT SHEET (page 61) with the Team.**

- **USE THIS PAGE TO PLAN THE "GET-TOGETHER" YOU WILL CONDUCT DURING WEEK 5:**

Date:_____ Time:_____ Place:_____

ACTIVITY	ASSIGNED TO:	REMARKS

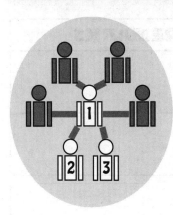

- PRAY! Ask the Lord to guide you as you choose the next person you will spend time with this week.
- Schedule an activity with ANOTHER Type "B" Unbeliever.
- Keep in touch with the persons you shared with in past weeks.
- Telephone each one of your Team members.
- Share the name of the persons and the times you will be with them this week.

SUGGESTIONS FOR YOUR ACTIVITY DURING THE "GET-TOGETHER"

- Ask the Lord to give you a GENUINE LOVE for each person!

- Spend your time with the GUESTS—not fellow Team members.

- Focus on LISTENING, not talking.

- Seek to understand the NEEDS and INTERESTS of each person.

- Consider ways you might MEET A NEED in each person's life.

Remember—being a SERVANT is the heart of reaching people!

PRACTICAL ASSIGNMENT

REPORT TO TEAM MEMBERS

WRITE IN THIS SPACE THOUGHTS YOU WISH TO SHARE WITH YOUR TEAM

- Your response to the first "Get-Together:"

- Prayer concerns about Type "B" Unbelievers:

- Insights which might help the Team in the ministry at this stage:

Each "Get-Together" will be sponsored and hosted by a different Team member. In each case, the primary purpose of the gathering is to develop friendships between the Type "B" Unbelievers and the other two Team members. It's important for you to focus on that objective.

PRAYER IS THE PRIMARY PREPARATION

There should be a season of prayer prior to each of these sessions. The host Team member should share as much as possible about the needs and the situations surrounding each person's life. This is, of course, not shared in the form of gossip, but rather for intercessory prayer. It is *crucial* that you keep such sharing strictly confidential!

Pray also that the Lord will give you knowledge about how you should minister to each person. You are not just socializing—you are bringing Good News. The first step in that process is being linked to God before you are linked to the Type "B" Unbeliever. You will then become a channel of His love and grace. Prayer is the key to all this!

THINK ABOUT THE SEATING ARRANGEMENT . . .

When there is a special function, the host or hostess always thinks about the *seating arrangement*. This ensures that people who will have things in common are together. As the host for your "Get-Together," you are the only one who knows both the Team members and your friends who have been invited. Therefore, give special attention to how people should be clustered. There may be as many as four or even five Type "B" Unbelievers who may attend. This means there could be seven or eight people present. Think about the clusters you wish to form, and instruct the Team members.

SELECT A CONVERSATIONAL SETTING

Avoid a room that must be used as a passageway by non-participating members of the family. If your own home seems inappropriate, perhaps you can meet in a private room in a restaurant, or in a place where you will not be disturbed.

If you meet outdoors, think about the comfort of the setting. Will there be too much sun, or too many bugs? If you are having a cookout, will the time involved in food preparation at the grill detract from the Team members being able to socialize? (If so, prepare the charcoal and the food well in advance of starting time.)

OVERCOME POTENTIAL DISTRACTIONS

Will some of the Type "B" Unbelievers be bringing their children along with them? If you also have children, you may end up spending a lot of time supervising them, never really free to concentrate on each other. In such cases, it is very wise to have a friend volunteer to take the children to a separate room or facility. In such cases, there should be careful preparation made for them, so the children from the Type "B" homes will want to have more contacts with your own children.

THINGS TO CONSIDER

- Avoid tall flowers in a vase placed to block the view of people sitting in a circle.

- Don't seat someone in a doorway where people may need to pass in or out.

- Be sure the room is the proper temperature. Trying to share in a hot and stuffy place makes people want to leave early.

- If you are having a mixed group, avoid seating men on one side of the room and the women on the other side. Let husbands and wives sit together.

- The distance between people when they are sharing strongly influences the conversation. Avoid two things: people sitting so close that they are uneasy, or people seated so far away from each other that they don't feel a sense of belonging together.

IT'S ALL A MATTER OF COMMON SENSE!

WEEK 4, DAY 2
THIS WEEK: BRIDGING THE GAP—SPONSORING "GET-TOGETHERS"
TODAY: THE "QUAKER QUESTIONS"

The topic for your three "Get-Togethers" should be *the people present*—nothing else! Whether they will take the form of a dinner party, a cookout, a barbeque, or perhaps even a birthday party, the primary purpose for the sessions is to bond relationships.

Years ago, a Quaker community in Indiana developed a set of questions used to welcome newcomers. All the neighbors would bring food with them, and they would share a common meal. Then, they used four questions to get acquainted. They are now called the "Quaker Questions."

They are extremely helpful in allowing people to become acquainted, without stirring up painful areas which would not be appropriate to share with strangers. To accomplish this, *the ages of 7 to 12* are selected as the time in life to be discussed. These childhood years are "safe" years for most people. While there may be some sad memories from these years, children usually are the victims, not the agents, of all events.

You will be delighted to see the way the questions reveal similarities of experiences, etc., between the people present. A natural bond begins to link people who find they have things in common: "You lived in *that* place? So did I! Did you know Joseph, whose father had a food shop?" Or, "My father was just like yours. I never saw him. He was always working . . . "

Each of the four questions deals with a slightly different area of life. The first one, as you will see, establishes the *home life* of each person during childhood years. The second one establishes the *economic lifestyle* of the family. The third refers to *emotional ties* during childhood. (Don't be surprised to discover people who had none!) The fourth refers in a general way to *the awareness of God.* Let's memorize them:

USE THIS EXACT WORDING WHEN PRESENTING THE "QUAKER QUESTIONS:"

The sponsor of the "Get-Together" begins by saying, "I have discovered four questions that were used 200 years ago to help people get acquainted with each other when they first met. Let's try them to get to know each other better. None of them pry into our private lives. We can answer each one before going on to the next one. I'll answer each one first:

"WHERE DID YOU LIVE BETWEEN THE AGES OF 7 AND 12, AND HOW MANY BROTHERS AND SISTERS WERE IN YOUR FAMILY?"

The time and detail you use when answering each question first will set the trend for everyone else. Take a full minute to answer. If you share your answers in some detail, others will do the same. Then, move on to the second question:

"WHAT TYPE OF TRANSPORTATION DID YOUR FAMILY USE?"

After all have shared the answer to this second question, comment about those who have had similar backgrounds. Then, present the third question:

"WHO WAS THE PERSON YOU FELT CLOSEST TO DURING THOSE YEARS?"

Be sensitive to the person who may say, "I really can't remember . . . " This may signal of some painful times which would not be shared with strangers. Then, present the fourth and last question:

"WHEN DID THE WORD "GOD" BEGIN TO HAVE SPECIAL MEANING FOR YOU?"

Team members may be able to share their own conversion experiences at this time, but be sure you do not get "preachy!" People have found special meaning in the word "God" in many different ways. *Just listen!* You will gain insights into why each person is Type "B."

Read Romans 5:8

In the illustration to the left, we have a picture of the way some Type "B" Unbelievers might act in a "Get-Together." Note the different ways they defend themselves from others who might try to get close to them.

Several issues are raised by this drawing. *First of all, circle the person you might dislike the most if you were sitting in that circle.*

Why did you ciricle that person? Why does that form of defensiveness cause you to react emotionally?

What would happen if you did, in fact, find yourself in a Share Group with a person like that? Could you do more harm than good by unconsciously registering your dislike?

You might also take a moment and think about which type of person *you* become when you become defensive. Which of these postures might *you* choose when you feel insecure?

WHY DO THESE PEOPLE ACT THIS WAY?

They are, without exception, *afraid!* Of what?

They are afraid of being "uncovered." They don't like themselves, or they don't feel they can compete with others. Perhaps they have been damaged by cruel acts and don't want to stand such pain again. They are all defensive *because they are afraid.*

As you become a friend to such persons, you must do what Jesus did: *look beyond their exteriors and see the inner pain which causes their conduct.* Remain prayerful and objective when you meet such people!

WEEK 4, DAY 4
THIS WEEK: BRIDGING THE GAP—SPONSORING "GET-TOGETHERS"
TODAY: "GATE-KEEPING"—OPENING AND SHUTTING

In the diagram to the right, a "Get-Together" is under way. The Quaker Questions have been shared, and now there is a general time of sharing taking place. It is not structured. People are just talking to each other.

Each lighter colored circle represents a person in the group. The darker circle represents comments thrown out for the entire group to consider. Each arrow indicates a person speaking. The arrows point to the person addressed.

There are many interesting things to note in this diagram. Let's consider some of them:

NOTE THE SILENT MEMBER IN THE GROUP

Why is this person not talking? More important, *who knows this is taking place?* As a good Team member, you should always be sensitive to those not sharing.

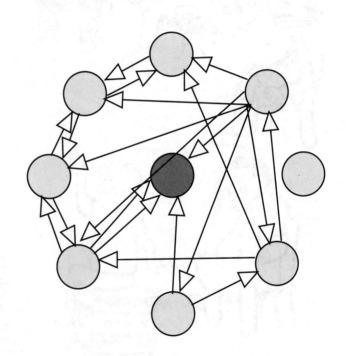

BE A "GATE-KEEPER" FOR THE SILENT PERSON

Consider this individual as one who needs "permission" to enter into the conversation. "Open the gate" by asking, "Stephen, what do *you* think about this?", or something similar. It's a terrible thing to be in a group where someone doesn't talk at all, and no one cares. There is a special feeling of being rejected that takes place in such circumstances. One of your greatest tasks is to constantly monitor the dynamics of the group and help the silent to share.

NOTE THE OVERTALKER IN THE GROUP

(This person is *obvious!)* What can you do about this? If you don't stop this domination, a feeling of uneasiness will develop and people will avoid your invitation to spend time in the Share Group where this must be endured! If you study the arrows, you will discover that the resentment of the group is shown by the lack of direct response to the overtalker. *Do something!*

BE A "GATE-SHUTTER" FOR THE OVERTALKER

This is a real skill, and one you will want to master as soon as possible. Every overtalker has to stop to take a breath. In that split second, shut the gate by asking someone else, "Rachel, what do *you* think about that?" Then, when Rachel has answered, once again briefly control the group by asking, "Jerome, do *you* have any thoughts about this?" Quite often, this may be enough to release the group from the feeling of being dominated.

OTHER INTERESTING THINGS ARE EVIDENT . . .

Note that some of the people are conversing only with their neighbors. Others are speaking across the room to people who are not seated next to them. Be alert to this tendency of people to create "subgroups." If it goes on too long, draw those involved into the larger context.

Note that the questions thrown out for the entire group to consider are not too frequent. This is because no one wants to be "in charge" of the group in this situation. As Team members, any one of you should feel free to ask the entire group a question. It's important that this be done through the session, or the bonding may begin to unravel. People may leave feeling they have gotten acquainted with one or two, but that the group as a whole is still filled with strangers.

WEEK 4, DAY 5
THIS WEEK: BRIDGING THE GAP—SPONSORING "GET-TOGETHERS"
TODAY: POST-MORTEM

After the "Get-Together" has ended, use the Evaluation Sheet at the right to review the session. *(If you take this book with you to the gathering, don't leave it laying around for your guests to read!)*

Undoubtedly you will have discovered many things you might have improved. While they are fresh in your minds, discuss the next "Get-Together." You will have opportunity to sharpen your skills.

HERE ARE SOME QUESTIONS TO THINK ABOUT AS YOU DO YOUR POST-EVALUATION:

1. WERE YOU ENCOURAGERS?
   Did you show warmth? Were you loving? Did you accept all persons as they were, without being judgmental?
2. DID YOU LISTEN?
   Did you hear and respect the ideas of others?

3. DID YOU HARMONIZE?
   Were you able to relieve potential conflicts in the group?

4. WERE YOU GATEKEEPERS?
   Did each Team member remain sensitive to the group dynamics which followed the sharing of the Quaker Questions? Did you do a good job of helping each person relate to others in the group?

5. WERE YOU INFORMATION SEEKERS?
   Did you ask questions which would draw from others their values and convictions?

6. DID YOU AVOID AN "US" (TEAM) VERSUS "THEM" ENVIRONMENT?
   Were you careful to mix well with them and not "hang together" as a Team? *Did they enjoy being with you? Did you enjoy being with them?*

"GET-TOGETHER" EVALUATION SHEET

IN THIS "GET-TOGETHER"...

(CIRCLE ONE CATEGORY FOR EACH STATEMENT)

LEADERSHIP WAS:	DOMINATED BY ONE PERSON	DOMINATED BY A SUBGROUP	CENTERED IN HALF THE GROUP	SHARED BY ALL THE MEMBERS
COMMUNICATION WAS:	BADLY BLOCKED	DIFFICULT	FAIRLY OPEN	VERY OPEN AND FREE
PEOPLE WERE:	PHONY	HIDDEN	FAIRLY OPEN	HONEST AND AUTHENTIC
THE TEAM WAS:	AVOIDING ITS TASK	LOAFING	GETTING SOME WORK DONE	WORKING HARD AT ITS TASK
I FELT:	MISUNDER-STOOD & REJECTED	SOMEWHAT MISUNDERSTOOD	SOMEWHAT ACCEPTED	COMPLETELY ACCEPTED & UNDERSTOOD BY THE GROUP

THE ONE WORD I WOULD USE TO DESCRIBE THE CLIMATE OF THIS MEETING:

_____

COUNTDOWN TO SHARE GROUP LAUNCH

WEEK 1: (Date)_____
Develop relationship with first Type "B" Unbeliever

WEEK 2: (Date)_____
Develop relationship with second Type "B" Unbeliever.

WEEK 3: (Date)_____
Develop relationship with third Type "B" Unbeliever.

WEEK 4: (Date)_____
Conduct first "Get-Together."

WEEK 5: (Date)_____
Conduct second "Get-Together."

WEEK 6: (Date)_____
Conduct third "Get-Together."

WEEK 7: (Date)_____
Each Team member invites two Type "B" Unbelievers to attend 10-week Share Group gatherings.

WEEK 8: (Date)_____
Team attends briefing for launching Share Group; Part 2, "Building Groups" manual is distributed.

WEEK 9: (Date)_____
Team shares in half night of prayer for their ministry.

WEEK 10: (Date)_____
SHARE GROUP LAUNCH

WEEK FOUR
CELL GROUP EQUIPPING TIME

THE TEAM SHARES...

UP TO 3 MINUTES PER PERSON:

- Team members share reports on working with "Type B" Unbelievers
- Share items you have noted on your REPORT SHEET (page75) with the Team.

- **USE THIS PAGE TO PLAN THE "GET-TOGETHER" YOU WILL CONDUCT DURING WEEK 5:**

Date:_____ **Time:**_____ **Place:**_____

ACTIVITY	ASSIGNED TO:	REMARKS

PRACTICAL ASSIGNMENT FOR WEEK FIVE:

PARTICIPATE IN THIS WEEK'S "GET-TOGETHER"

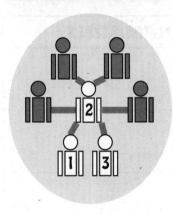

- PRAY! Ask the Lord to guide you as you choose the next person you will spend time with this week.
- Schedule an activity with ANOTHER Type "B" Unbeliever.
- Keep in touch with the persons you shared with in past weeks.
- Telephone each one of your Team members.
- Share the name of the persons and the times you will be with them this week.

SUGGESTIONS FOR YOUR ACTIVITY DURING THIS "GET-TOGETHER"

- Evaluate your effectiveness in last week's event. How can you be more responsive to the Guests this week?
- Spend your time with the GUESTS—not fellow Team members.
- Remember to focus on LISTENING, not talking.
- How do the NEEDS and INTERESTS of these new people match up with those you met last week?
- What follow-up ministry can you sense the Lord wants you to do as a result of getting to know these persons?

WRITE IN THIS SPACE THOUGHTS YOU WISH TO SHARE WITH YOUR TEAM

- Report on your contacts this week:

- Evaluation of the last "Get-Together:"

- Special prayer requests:

Read Matthew 12:34-35

THERE ARE TWO LEVELS TO COMMUNICATION

1. The "Get-acquainted" Level

Can you imagine someone you barely know asking you: "How much money do you have in the bank?" Sounds riduculous, doesn't it?

There are certain things which aren't discussed between people who are at the "Get-acquainted" Level. One of those things *(for many people)* is their relationship to God.

One must *earn the right* to discuss such personal things. At the "Get-Acquainted" Level, there is a search for common ground. Once it is found, a *Trust Level* is created which permits *some* things to be discussed.

Have you ever wondered why it takes only ten minutes for you to establish a good relationship with one person, and with others it takes hours, weeks, or even *months?* One reason is that when two people meet for the first time, there are *nine ways* they may react to each other:

+ + Each person reacts positively to the other
+ - Positive response meets a negative response
+ 0 Positive response meets a neutral response
- - Negative response meets a negative response
- + Negative response meets a positive response
- 0 Negative response meets a neutral response
0 + Neutral response meets a positive response
0 - Neutral response meets a negative response
0 0 Neutral response meets a neutral response

People also react in a certain way because of the special set of problems they may be facing at the time they meet. We must remember that our servant ministry requires us to understand each person, so we may minister to them. At this "Get-acquainted Level," the question we must answer must be:

"HOW CAN THIS PERSON BE SHOWN THE LORD JESUS CHRIST, AND HEALED BY HIS LOVE AND POWER?"

By *listening,* the way to open the door to "Deep Trust" levels will be discovered. In the meantime, pray much for the person...and let the Holy Spirit guide you! When you have *earned the right* to talk about more intimate truths, the Outsider will truly welcome the discussion. You'll be glad you waited.

2. The "Deep Trust" Level

"TRUST: Reliance on the integrity or justice of a person; confidence in the ability or intention of a person; a person that one relies on."

At this level, two people feel free to share important things with each other. It is also at this level that Christ will be revealed most clearly through your closely examined life style. Therefore, spending time with your Type "B" Outsider friend is the key to developing a level where deep trust can take place.

Here's a modern problem your Team must solve: *Our relationships are too superficial to adequately reveal Jesus Christ.* The occasional visit from a stranger is not enough to win the lost. As a result of time spent together, confidence in a person develops. Trust leads to a willingness to share the *real* reasons for Christ not being accepted as Lord. Remember to keep your priorities straight, and to . . .
KEEP THE MAIN THING THE MAIN THING!

"FRED, I'D LIKE TO COME — BUT I'VE RESERVED THAT TIME TO BE WITH ONE OF MY UNBELIEVING FRIENDS!"

WEEK 5, DAY 2
THIS WEEK: BRIDGING THE GAP—GOOD COMMUNICATION
TODAY: IMPACT COMMUNICATION

"IMPACT COMMUNICATION" OCCURS AT THE "DEEP TRUST" LEVEL

"IMPACT COMMUNICATION" is a term which occurs only at the level of deepest trust. It occurs when two people are sharing as trusting friends. It takes place when the Type "B" Unbeliever is touched by Christ's love in an unexpected way.

EXAMPLE: A Type "B" woman whose marriage had unexpectedly dissolved went into a deep depression. She met the Share Group team at a "Get-Acquainted" party, and agreed to join the 10-week Share Group.

There, she began to gain insights into her problems. Her life was changed. As a result, she later was reunited to her husband, and both accepted Christ.

In this case, IMPACT COMMUNICATION was in the form of hours of interaction with the Share Group Team members. If she had not met the Team, she might have been a suicide.

EXAMPLE: A man dying of cancer was asked by a well-meaning Christian: "You speak openly of dying. Are you ready to meet your Maker?"

The sick man responded with anger, "You Christians disgust me. If your God is so loving, why does He cause me to leave my wife and daughter penniless when I die?" The Christian left the conversation humiliated by his insensitivity.

Soon, he returned. This time, he came to offer full employment for the wife. He had asked a fellow Cell Group member to sell the house without collecting a realtor's fee. He offered to make all further payments on the home, so the family could be together. The house

92

would be sold only *after* the man had passed away, and offered to help the wife invest the profit from the sale. He also volunteered the members of his Cell Group to assist the wife in moving the furniture to a lovely apartment he had secured for her.

The dying man wept with relief, thanking the Christian for his assistance. In this case, the "Gospel" was the good news that Christians would care for his widow and his daughter after his death. In the hospital, shortly before he passed away, he gave his life to Christ. His wife, also a Type "B" Unbeliever, also became a Christian and the daughter became active for the Lord.

"IMPACT COMMUNICATION" ALWAYS INVOLVES TWO FACTORS . . .

1. *IT IS UNPREDICTABLE.*
    When one knows what language will be used, or what conclusions will be reached *in advance,* the IMPACT is ZERO!

2. *IT TOUCHES DIRECTLY ON THE PROBLEM.*
    In the second example, the Christian *thought* the greatest concern of the dying man would be where he would spend eternity. It wasn't!

Upon his return, the Share Group Team member touched the deepest heart need of the man. The IMPACT was made by serving the man at the point of his greatest worry.

As you get acquainted with the Type "B" Unbelievers during these weeks, realize that the gospel comes to people by meeting their needs. Often our *assumptions* that their deepest needs have to do with going to heaven or hell when they die are not accurate.

DISTINGUISH BETWEEN FELT NEEDS AND REAL NEEDS

We must always distinguish between *felt needs* and *real needs.* While as Christians we know the real need of the unbeliever is to know our Lord, this may not be a topic to discuss until a close relationship has been established. Then, the means of revealing Christ must unpredictably touch upon the *felt need* of the individual.

It is for this reason we must be alert to the way the power of God can touch unbelievers. If we pray for the healing or deliverance of an unbeliever, the results may be not only a physical or spiritual healing, but also the way to bring the person to follow our Lord!

WEEK 5, DAY 3
THIS WEEK: BRIDGING THE GAP—GOOD COMMUNICATION
TODAY: SUMMARY OF COMMUNICATION ZONES—1

REVIEW THESE FOUR TYPES OF COMMUNICATION ZONES (More on this tomorrow . . .)

SHARING

Mutual respect exists.

Two-way comunication is possible.

Asking, answering is taking place.

A joint search for truth takes place.

Discussions are marked by patience and love.

Lets the *Holy Spirit* draw, rather than trying to coerce.

Develops common acceptance of Scripture as a jointly accepted authority about God's plan for mankind.

RULING

One person dominates.

Assumes "My ideas are right, my approaches best!"

Imposes one point of view on other person.

Conveys lack of respect for the other person or other beliefs held.

Insensitive to needs or problems faced by other person.

Breeds anger, fear, or hostility.

GIVE IN

Shifts the issue to the ruling person.

Assumes other person knows or can contribute more.

Makes few contributions of own ideas.

Does not have any feeling of "ownership" of agreed-upon solutions.

Willing to let *others* assume responsibility.

S-P-L-I-T

Withdrawal—total and complete!

May be marked by fear or anger.

A feeling that nothing more can be done.

No further contribution to the friendship is offered or desired.

There is a deliberate avoidance of the relationship.

	INFORM		EXPLORE
	"Let's consider the possibility . . ."		"What do you think about . . ."
	"Here's an additional thought . . ."	**SHARING**	How long have you felt . . ."
	"I recently read . . ."		I'd like to understand . . ."
	Perhaps this might help . . ."		Tell me about . . ."

INFORM — "Let's consider the possibility . . ." / "Here's an additional thought . . ." / "I recently read . . ." / Perhaps this might help . . ."

SHARING

EXPLORE — "What do you think about . . ." / How long have you felt . . ." / I'd like to understand . . ." / Tell me about . . ."

RULE

PERSUADE
"I really feel I am right . . ."
"You really should go along . . ."
"It's absolutely necessary for you to . . ."
"You should not delay to . . ."

ENFORCE
"Hell is ahead, unless you . . ."
"If you don't do this, the results will be . . ."
"I must insist you realize the consequences if . . ."

CONTROLLING

GIVE IN

ACCOMMODATE
"Let's try it your way . . ."
"If you really feel that's best . . ."
"I'll trust your opinions . . ."

COMPLY
"I'm not in agreement, but . . ."
"I don't want to stick MY neck out . . ."
"I'll agree to do it to solve a problem . . ."
"Well, the only way to get along is to go along . . ."

FIGHT
"I've forgotten the problem.
   Now, I'm angry at YOU . . ."
"This has become personal now . . ."
"Who do you think you are, anyhow? . . ."
"You have no right to . . ."

SPLITTING

FLIGHT
"I just want to get away . . ."
"I'm too busy to see you . . ."
"I'd like to drop this, please . . ."
"There's no use in more talking . . ."

Take a few minutes to review the presentation of Communication Zones on pages 94 and 95.

HOW COMMUNICATION PROGRESSES

Study the patterns of communication that flow from the top left to the bottom left on the graph on page 95. Do you see how they are *aggressive*, from . . .

- INFORMING to . . .

- PERSUADING to . . .

- ENFORCING to . . .

- FIGHT!

Now, consider the *passive form* of communication that flow from the top right to the bottom right of the graph. List the progression you observe there:

- _____ to . . .

- _____ to . . .

- _____ to . . .

- _____!

A deteriorating relationship will often proceed along these lines. This is why a Share Group Team should be careful to keep the communication level at the *very top*, in the "WE SHARE" Zone!

LET'S DISCOVER HOW JESUS COMMUNICATED

Read John 4:7, 9-18:

This passage is significant! Jesus' patterns of communication with the woman He met at Jacob's well are classic examples of powerful communication.

1. The IMPACT communication in this conversation happens in verse 16. After studying the passage, explain why Jesus made an impact by what He said:

_____

_____

_____

_____

2. How many times does Jesus speak to the woman before He makes the "IMPACT" statement?

2   4   6   8

3. A "PERSUADE" statment occurs in verse 15. It was Jesus' clue that the woman had accepted Him on a "DEEP TRUST" level. Explain why her statement, in your opinion, gave Him this clue:

_____

_____

_____

_____

_____

As you relate to others, sensitize yourself to Type "B" Unbelievers who are now relating to you on a "GET ACQUAINTED" Level, and those who are relating on a 'DEEP TRUST" Level.

WEEK 5, DAY 5
THIS WEEK: BRIDGING THE GAP—GOOD COMMUNICATION
TODAY: SUMMARY OF COMMUNICATION ZONES—3

HOW JESUS HANDLED A FLIGHT PATTERN

Read John 4:16-29

1. The reaction of the woman to the statement of Jesus was to "change the subject." IN WHAT VERSE DOES THIS HAPPEN?

_____

2. What subject does she choose to discuss? Why do you suppose she chose this topic?

_____

_____

_____

3. How does Jesus respond?
   (Underline your answers)

He tells her to stick to the original subject.

He brings up a different topic.

He "flows" with her, discussing the subject she chose.

He realizes she has been threatened by His clear knowledge of her lifestyle, and His revelation of it.

He presses her for immediate repentance from her wicked lifestyle.

He recognizes He must not destroy her dignity, and gently follows her diversion for the sake of the relationship.

4. The answer of Jesus to the woman's change of subject is significant, due to its unusual length (verses 21-24). Below are some possible reasons for this long answer. Which ones do you think apply? *(Check the box of your choice:)*

☐ A. A short, quick answer might have communicated a lack of acceptance.

☐ B. Her respect for Him provided a teaching time.

☐ C. Both of the above answers are correct.

☐ D. Neither of the above answers are correct.

5. While B above might be true, it is also possible that she was so threatened by what Jesus knew about her that she did not truly "listen" to his long explanation. *His answer was long because He was affirming her.* In spite of all He knew, He treated her with respect—as an equal. Look at verse 29: *What did she remember most about His words to her?*

_____

_____

6. Can you think of a situation when you were affirmed by someone "talking things out" with you? When?

_____

_____

_____

_____

_____

_____

REMEMBER JESUS' WAY OF HANDLING A FLIGHT PATTERN. YOU'LL FIND IT USEFUL!

COUNTDOWN TO SHARE GROUP LAUNCH

WEEK 1: (Date)_____
Develop relationship with first Type "B" Unbeliever

WEEK 2: (Date)_____
Develop relationship with second Type "B" Unbeliever.

WEEK 3: (Date)_____
Develop relationship with third Type "B" Unbeliever.

WEEK 4: (Date)_____
Conduct first "Get-Together."

WEEK 5: (Date)_____
Conduct second "Get-Together."

WEEK 6: (Date)_____
Conduct third "Get-Together."

WEEK 7: (Date)_____
Each Team member invites two Type "B" Unbelievers to attend 10-week Share Group gatherings.

WEEK 8: (Date)_____
Team attends briefing for launching Share Group; Part 2, "Building Groups" manual is distributed.

WEEK 9: (Date)_____
Team shares in half night of prayer for their ministry.

WEEK 10: (Date)_____
SHARE GROUP LAUNCH

WEEK FIVE
CELL GROUP EQUIPPING TIME

THE TEAM SHARES...

UP TO 3 MINUTES PER PERSON:

- Spend time in prayer for the next "Get-Together"
- Share items from your REPORT SHEETS (page 89) with one another.

■ USE THIS PAGE TO RECORD PRAYER REQUESTS ABOUT THE TYPE "B" UNBELIEVERS YOUR TEAM MATES ARE CULTIVATING:

NAME OF PERSON:	TEAM MEMBER:	REMARKS:

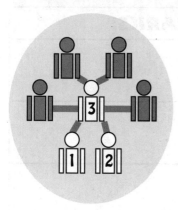

- PRAY! Ask the Lord to guide you as you choose the next person you will spend time with this week.
- Schedule an activity with a Type "B" Unbeliever.
- Keep in touch with the persons you shared with in past weeks.
- Telephone each one of your Team members.
- Share the name of the persons and the times you will be with them this week.

SUGGESTIONS FOR YOUR ACTIVITY DURING THIS "GET-TOGETHER"

- Evaluate your effectiveness in last week's event. How can you be more responsive to the Guests this week?

- Spend your time with the GUESTS—not fellow Team members.

- Remember to focus on LISTENING, not talking.

- How do the NEEDS and INTERESTS match up with those you met in the previous "Get-Togethers?"

- What follow-up ministry can you sense the Lord wants you to do as a result of getting to know these persons?

PRACTICAL ASSIGNMENT

REPORT TO TEAM MEMBERS

WRITE IN THIS SPACE THOUGHTS YOU
WISH TO SHARE WITH YOUR TEAM

- Report on your contacts this week:

- Evaluation of the last "Get-Together:"

- Special prayer requests:

WEEK 6, DAY 1
THIS WEEK: BRIDGING THE GAP—HANDLING DISTORTIONS
TODAY: DISCERNING LEVEL 5 AND 4 COMMENTS

Review the Pyramid on page 8.

As you share with TYpe "B" Unbelievers, you should be able to classify their remarks. It is by the shift in comments made that you will be able to discern their responsiveness. Here's an exercise to help you think about the "Levels" revealed by different comments.

AT WHAT LEVEL IS A PERSON WHO SAYS:

THIS PERSON IS AT LEVEL . . .				
1	2	3	4	5

EXAMPLE: "Please show me how I can be born again; I'm ready!" — X (Level 1)

1. "Do you think there is a God?"
2. "Why are you a Christian?"
3. "Are all you Christians really 'on the level'?"
4. "I think everyone will go to heaven!"
5. "Why should I believe in God?"
6. "Must I become a Christian now?"
7. "Religion is for weak people who can't handle their problems."
8. "What did Christ mean when He said..."
9. "Is there anything wrong with an occasional drink?"
10. "How does the Bible help you solve your problems?"

AT WHAT LEVEL WOULD YOU ASK THESE QUESTIONS?

EXAMPLE: "Would you like to join a Bible Study Group?"

1. "How do you think the world was created?"
2. "Do you feel that you are a part of the Christian community?"
3. "I'd like to tell you the greatest thing that ever happened to me!"
4. "What do you believe about Jesus Christ?"
5. "May I show you how to receive Christ into your life?"
6. "Do you think you'd lose your friends if you accepted Christ?"
7. "Have you attended church in the past year?"
8. "Do you understand why Christians go to church?"
9. "In your opinion, who is Jesus Christ?"
10. "Do you understand the Bible?"

THIS PERSON IS AT LEVEL . . .				
1	2	3	4	5
	X			

ANSWERS: Page 104—1: 5; 2: 3 or 2; 3: 4 or 5; 4: 5; 5: 5; 6: 3 or 2; 7: 5; 8: 2 or 1; 9: who knows?; 10: 2 or 3.
Page 105—1: 3 to 5; 2: 3; 3: 4 or 5; 4: 3 to 5; 5: 2 or 1; 6: 3 or 4; 7: 3 to 5; 8: 3 to 5; 9: 5; 10: 2 to 5.

105

In understanding the Type "B" Unbeliever's response to what we share with them, we must distinguish between PAST EXPERIENCES and PRESENT EXPERIENCING.

MISSING DETAILS are filled in from PAST EXPERIENCES.

EXPERIENCING takes place only in the PRESENT.

The moment we experience something, it becomes a part of our life, stored up as a PAST EXPERIENCE.

Then, as a PAST EXPERIENCE, it causes us to respond in a new way to PRESENT EXPERIENCES.

The more INPUT we provide to those who have a distorted picture of the Gospel, the more PAST EXPERIENCES they will store up, which helps them to respond positively to Jesus Christ.

CONTINUED EXPOSURE TO CHRIST IS AN IMPORTANT FACTOR IN HELPING PEOPLE COME TO KNOW JESUS CHRIST

Paul said in 2 Corinthians 3:3:

> ". . . you are a letter that has come from Christ . . . .a letter written not with ink but with the Spirit of the Living God written not on stone tablets but on the pages of the human heart."

Do you see once more how *important* time is as a factor in reaching Type "B" Unbelievers? It is obvious that we cannot spend much time with dozens of people. True! But, since the *greatest number* of people are at levels 3, 4, and 5, is it not important for the future harvest for you to spend time with them?

EXPLANATION:

Stored in the memory banks of each person are all sorts of past experiences. These are represented in this illustration by the many symbols in the brain area. Among those symbols is a star and a check mark. When a new experience occurs, the person "filters" the past memories of such experiences.

INPUT

The RESPONSE is not "pure." It reflects all sorts of good or bad encounters with experiences in the past.

For this reason, you must not be surprised when a fairly simple issue becomes complicated by a Type "B" Unbeliever. They are "programmed" to respond in ways which may be unexpected by you. Their reaction is not only to the current event, but to things in the past.

INPUT

RESPONSE

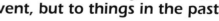

107

WEEK 6, DAY 3
THIS WEEK: BRIDGING THE GAP—HANDLING DISTORTIONS
TODAY: RESULT OF IGNORING TRUTH

Read Mark 7:1-23

1. Jesus said of the Pharisee, "You ignore the

   commandment of _____

   and instead you teach the _____ of

   men."

2. What was the commandment which the Pharisees
   ignored? *(v. 10)*

   _____

   _____

   _____

   _____

3. What was the distortion they were teaching?
   (v. 11-13)

   _____

   _____

   _____

   _____

4. Below are some examples of how the Bible is distorted. In each case, a truth must be ignored in order that the distortion can occur.

Draw a line from each distortion in the left column to the particular truth in the right column which has been ignored, or is unknown:

"Christianity is just a bunch of rules."	"Christ has redeemed us from the curse of the law."
"Sure, I am a Christian. I believe in God."	
	"Lift up your eyes; the fields are white!"
"I'm not good enough to be a Christian."	
	"While we were yet sinners, Christ died for us."
"People really don't want to hear about Jesus."	
	"All our righteousness is as filthy rags."

WEEK 6, DAY 4
THIS WEEK: BRIDGING THE GAP—HANDLING DISTORTIONS
TODAY: SAUL OF TARSUS

Read Mark 7:1-23

Saul of Tarsus is a classic example of a very sincere person who has totally distorted reality. He caused much pain and suffering among the people of God. *However, at the time he felt he was doing the right thing!*

1. According to 8:1, how determined was Paul to destroy the new Christian movement?

   _____

   _____

   _____

   _____

2. Consider: have you ever been so obsessed by a strong conviction that you would be willing to help *kill* other people? If so, note the circumstances:

   _____

   _____

   _____

   _____

3. Put yourself in Paul's shoes: *why did he have such deep resentment against Christians?* What did they threaten which was precious to Paul?

   _____

   _____

   _____

   _____

4. The way Stephen died "pricked" Paul's heart. Later, God would say to him, "It's hard for you to kick against the goads!" *Why was Stephen's death such a powerful witness to Paul?*

_____

_____

_____

_____

5. Consider a Type "B" Outsider you know who scoffs at things of God. *What will have to be experienced before he or she would turn to Christ?*

_____

_____

_____

_____

Are distortions often cleared up by the impact of a Christian life? Can you think of some true examples of this you have observed or experienced?

HOW DISTORTED ARE YOUR MOTIVES FOR BEING INVOLVED IN THIS SHARE GROUP MINISTRY?

Read Galatians 3:1-3

Paul's frustration with the Christians in Galatia was because they had distorted the truth they had been taught by him. He had led them to understand that the Holy Spirit was the source of their power, their victory, their *everything*. However, they had turned away from the source of power. They had focused on keeping the Jewish Law, thinking their *activities* were necessary to please God.

Paul is greatly distressed! His letter to them calls them to stop *doing things* for the Lord, and to realize they are "crucified with Christ" and did not need to judge their significance by their performance.

As you minister to unbelievers, always remember that the only thing you can be for them is the bearer of God's mighty power and love!

ARE YOU PROVIDING A "CLEAR PICTURE" OF CHRIST'S LOVE?

If you are simply becoming "one more friend" to the Type "B" Unbelievers, the impact of your witness for Christ will be distorted. In addition to being a *friend,* you should desire to be the instrument of God's Holy Spirit in their lives. Don't be afraid to share not only the *message,* but also the *power* of Christ. Pray for the sick. Pray in the presence of Unbeliever, whether they believe in what you are doing or not!

On the following page is an analysis of the ministry you have performed thus far. The evaluation you make of yourself should be made prayerfully.

HOW DO I LOOK TO TYPE "B" UNBELIEVERS?

- Do I communicate a genuine *love* for each person? Am I seen as caring about those who cannot do anything for me in return? Does my love contrast with the selfishness of those who use others for their own profit?

- Do I display an inner *joy* in my mannerisms? Do people enjoy seeing me enter the room? Does my joy contrast with those who are always moping, always frustrated with life?

- Is there a *peace* in my bearing? Jesus said I am to offer "my peace" to those who don't have it. Do I have an obvious peace about my bearing that would make others desire to receive the One who has given it to me? Does it contrast with the inner stress which fills the lives of Type "B" Unbelievers?

- Am I *patient* when I face stressful situations? Does my patience contrast with the testiness shown by those who are not pleased with their life's circumstances? When others might reveal an explosive character, do I remain calm?

- Do I reveal a spirit of *kindness* when I am with others? When someone makes a mistake, do I show a spirit of benevolence to them, instead of being rude to them?

- Is there a *goodness* about my life which is noticed by unbelievers? Is my modesty when around the opposite sex evident? Is my avoidance of dirty jokes and filthy language evident? Do others want to have this same dignity in their character?

- Am I viewed as *faithful?* Do I honor commitments and schedule arrangements? Do I pay my bills on time?

- Am I *gentle* with others? Am I sensitive to others?

- Do I display *self-control?* When the unexpected happens, do I react defensively to the circumstance, or does Christ continue to display His life within me? Do my family members admire my ability to handle quick shifts without revealing a crabby spirit?

"But the fruit of the Spirit is love, joy, peace, patience, kindness, goodness, faithfulness, gentleness, self-control; against such things there is no law . . . if we live by the Spirit, let us also walk by the Spirit." (Galatians 5:22-25)

113

COUNTDOWN TO SHARE GROUP LAUNCH

WEEK 1: (Date)_____
Develop relationship with first Type "B" Unbeliever

WEEK 2: (Date)_____
Develop relationship with second Type "B" Unbeliever.

WEEK 3: (Date)_____
Develop relationship with third Type "B" Unbeliever.

WEEK 4: (Date)_____
Conduct first "Get-Together."

WEEK 5: (Date)_____
Conduct second "Get-Together."

WEEK 6: (Date)_____
Conduct third "Get-Together."

WEEK 7: (Date)_____
Each Team member invites two Type "B" Unbelievers to attend 10-week Share Group gatherings.

WEEK 8: (Date)_____
Team attends briefing for launching Share Group; Part 2, "Building Groups" manual is distributed.

WEEK 9: (Date)_____
Team shares in half night of prayer for their ministry.

WEEK 10: (Date)_____
SHARE GROUP LAUNCH

WEEK SIX
CELL GROUP EQUIPPING TIME

THE TEAM SHARES...

UP TO 3 MINUTES PER PERSON:

- **Team members share reports on working with "Type B" Unbelievers**
- **Share items from your REPORT SHEETS (page 103) with one another.**

▪ USE THIS PAGE TO RECORD PRAYER REQUESTS ABOUT THE TYPE "B" UNBELIEVERS YOUR TEAM MATES ARE CULTIVATING:

NAME OF PERSON:	TEAM MEMBER:	REMARKS:

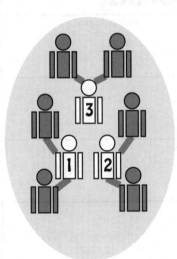

- PRAY! Ask the Lord to guide you as you invite Type "B" Unbelievers you have been cultivating to join you and your Team for a 10-week Share Group experience.
- VISIT each person you are going to invite. Don't try to do this by telephone. Make the invitation SPECIAL!
- In advance, develop THREE REASONS why the Share Group would have special value to each person you visit. Remember—people respond to invitations based upon whether it will meet a personal need.

PREPARING YOURSELF FOR THE TASK . . .

- Jesus prayed all night before selecting His twelve disciples. Even so, make your selection of those to invite a serious matter of prayer.
- Your goal: enlist TWO people to participate in the Share Group as your guest. You won't have time to minister effectively to more than two people during the 10-week Share Group period.
- As your Team mates share the names of those they have confirmed as participants, phone each one and let them know you are truly looking forward to the time you will be together.

WRITE IN THIS SPACE THOUGHTS YOU WISH TO SHARE WITH YOUR TEAM

- Report on those who will be joining you for the 10-week Share Group experience:

- Evaluation of the last "Get-Together:"

- Special prayer requests:

WEEK 7, DAY 1
THIS WEEK: FORMING YOUR SHARE GROUP
TODAY: ENLISTING TYPE "B" UNBELIEVERS

MAKE PRAYER YOUR FIRST PRIORITY

Perhaps you have already done so, but during this week *for sure* you should enlist your two guests for the Share Group. By this time, all of the Team have been introduced to all of those who are possibilities. Perhaps you have been cultivating three or more of your own Type "B" friends from your Oikos: now, seek the Lord about the ones to invite to participate.

Make the prayer time about this matter your very highest priority. Have a strong sense of being led by the Lord as you make each visit.

Expect to engage in spiritual warfare as you pray over this matter. Satan is not going to enjoy your snatching his captives from their strong prison cells of unbelief and blindness to God's love! Pray much, and keep your heart close to Him.

WHAT TO SAY WHEN INVITING YOUR GUESTS

Your conversation should take place face-to-face, and not be pressured or rushed. The actual wording you use should be your own choice, but the sincerity of your manner will mean more than the words.

Cover these points:

- Our time together during these past weeks has made a real impact on my life. I have enjoyed our friendship and the "Get-Togethers" we have shared.

- Using the names of your Team members, say something like this: "Stephen, Mary and I have wanted to form a group for getting together on a regular basis with some of our friends. We decided we would each invite two others to join us. So the group would have nine people—small enough for us to enjoy each other, and easy to move from house to house. I decided to invite you to join us, if you're interested."

> **NOTE: Do NOT say, "We are forming a Share Group which is sponsored by our church," or similar words. Your Share Group is YOUR MINISTRY, and not just a "program" of a church! Preserve the integrity of your relationship. There are no "hidden agendas," nothing to join, no dues, etc.**

- "We thought we would plan it for ten weeks. I'm sure we'll not all be able to come every time, but that's okay. Ten weeks will be long enough for us to really become close friends, and after that we can get together when we want to."

- "We haven't decided on the time for us to meet. We thought we might get together and find a time when everyone will be free most of the time."

- "We don't really need an agenda. The agenda will be 'US!' We can decide what we want to share about when we get together. And, by moving around and having it in different homes or restaurants, we can have a great time together. We thought we might start in two to three weeks."

- "If you'd like to be a part of our share group times, you are invited!"

- Those who are interested will quickly respond. If you get a negative response from someone, say, "That's okay! Maybe one week you might be free—let me know and you are welcome to just "drop in" and visit us." Keep the way open for continued contact with each person who declines.

- Let the two who accept know that you will be getting back soon to work out a time for the meetings.

- Then, send each one a greeting card with a friendship message on it, noting that you are looking forward to the times together.

- Continue to meet with each of these persons on a one-to-one basis in the interim until your Team launches the first group meeting.

WEEK 7, DAY 2
THIS WEEK: FORMING YOUR SHARE GROUP
TODAY: GUIDELINES FOR MEETINGS

FREQUENCY

Share Groups must meet weekly. Biweekly groups have never been effective. Groups meet in the evenings, mornings, noontimes during lunch breaks—*any time.* However, they should never conflict with the Cell Group that sponsors them, or when the Body of Christ meets to celebrate and worship.

TIME

Team members should agree both on the *starting* and the *closing* times. This enables members to arrange for baby sitters, etc. Meetings usually last for 1 1/2 hours, never more than 2 hours. *This includes snack time.* Do not let the Share Group last too long—you will lose members!

120

PLACE(S)

Unless you are meeting during a lunch break, always rotate the gathering, going from house to house. It's a good idea to hold the first meeting in the home of a Type "B" Unbeliever, since all of your own homes have already been used. Give them a feeling of "ownership" by doing this. You will discover why Acts 2:42 stresses the importance of doing this.

SIZE

The best size for a Share Group is nine people—three Team members, and six Type "B" Unbelievers. If the Team has four members, then there should be eight Type "B" Unbelievers, for a total of 12. That should be the absolute maximum. If occasional friends of the Type "B" Unbelievers wish to come, be sure you *never* go beyond 15 persons.

PRESIDERS

Each week, the members of the group rotate presiding over the meeting. If possible, let the Type "B" Unbelievers also preside in turn. *(Your opportunity to share or witness is not at all curtailed by doing this.)* It's important to remember that a Presider is *NOT* a teacher, and *NOT* a leader! Instead, this person is simply a catalyst to get the discussion under way. Formal control of a Share Group stifles the effectiveness.

AGENDA

As shown on the right, the agenda for the Share Group is very different from the Cell Group meeting you belong to. You will be given more guidance about this in the next book, *BUILDING GROUPS*. Refreshments are a part of the "Ice Breaking" *(dark shading)* time. Content time will be decided by the entire group, and will be explained to you in the next Briefing for Share Groups *(see Countdown Calendar).*

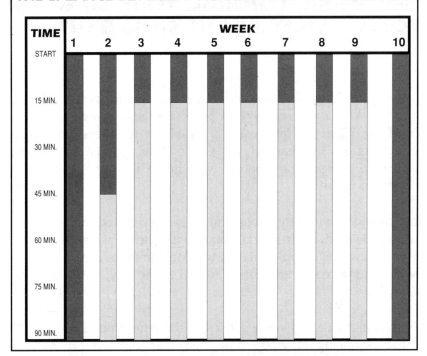

THE BALANCE BETWEEN "ICE BREAKING" AND CONTENT

OUTLINE OF TIME USE IN A SHARE GROUP

During the "Ice Breaker," refreshments are served.
Each session closes with a brief word of prayer.

WEEK 7, DAY 3
THIS WEEK: FORMING YOUR SHARE GROUP
TODAY: WHAT ABOUT CHILDREN?

Many Share Group Teams work with couples who have children. What an opportunity to penetrate those being raised by Type "B" families! It's important for these youngsters to be reached for Christ. Having them participate in the Share Group activity can be a valuable ministry to them!

Your agenda for a Share Group can be easily adapted to include children, with special ministry to them taking place during "big people's talk time." Most important is for the youngsters to know they are not in the way, but dearly loved.

Let the children assist in the serving of the refreshments at the beginning of group time. They can serve the cookies, hand out glasses of punch, etc. This gives them a feeling that they are participants in the group's life.

A very meaningful thing to do with them is to play a "Get-Acquainted Game" with them. Have the children sit in a circle, facing outward. Then have the adults sit in a larger circle, facing them. Until the game is finished, have one or two adults sit facing one child. The children tell their age, and then the adults share with the children what life was like for them at that age.

The generation gap between adults and children makes this a fascinating revelation to the youngsters. The difference in TV (or lack of it), radio, restaurants (did anyone live before there were fast foods?), and political conditions can be shared. Children quickly identify with adults who share such details!

More important, bonds are developed between each adult and each child in this way. For children being raised in homes where there may be great conflict and where Christ is never mentioned, these relationships have long-term value.

PLAN FOR A SPECIAL ACTIVITY FOR CHILDREN DURING "BIG PEOPLE'S TALK TIME."

Your Team can prepare ten sessions for the children, and rotate between yourselves being with the children. This cuts down the number of Team members in the adult sessions, of course, but it's important to weigh the total ministry opportunity. From time to time, Share Group Teams are able to invite one of the Cell Group members to work with the children in the group for the 10 week period. This can be a meaningful ministry for a new believer who has recently entered the cell group.

Creative things are possible, don't take a lot of work, and can have great impact on the children. Because they have great imaginations, a few "props" set up in another room of the home, or out of doors, can bring Bible stories alive.

Here are some suggestions:

1. ADAM AND EVE IN THE GARDEN
Let the children role-play the creation of Adam and then Eve, the taking of the fruit, and explaining that "sin" is not just doing something *bad,* but choosing deliberately to disobey God's loving directions.

2. EVENTS FROM THE LIVES OF BIBLE PEOPLE

Examples: Abraham and Isaac at the mountain, where God provided a lamb as a sacrifice for the son; Shadrack, Meshack, and Abednego in the fiery furnace; David and Goliath; the Crucifixion; the Resurrection; the conversion of Paul.

Creativity is the only limitation to what the children can learn by role playing and excursions outside the place where adults are meeting. Recently, one Team member dressed like Abraham and took the children on the trip across the "Fertile Crescent" from his homeland to Israel, burying his father on the way. They "journeyed" down streets and crossed a bridge, etc., with each landmark given a Bible name. Imagine the children passing by those places in the weeks that followed—recalling again the events connected to them!

BECOME "FAMILY" TO EACH CHILD

Ask each child to call you "Uncle" or "Aunt." Let them know you love them, and that you welcome times to listen to them tell about their lives, their toys, and eventually, their fears. The ministry of the Share Group to them may have eternal repercussions!

WEEK 7, DAY 4
THIS WEEK: FORMING YOUR SHARE GROUP
TODAY: SCRATCHING WHERE THEY ITCH

During these past weeks, you have gained insights into the *interests* and *problems* of your Type "B" Unbeliever friends. Now, it's time to think about the TOPICS you might suggest which would appeal to them.

Consider each lifestyle. What topics might be of value to each person? And, which topics might be of interest to *both* persons you will be bringing, even though it might not be top priority for both?

Perhaps you could chat with each person privately. Ask, "I've been thinking of some topics we might enjoy sharing about. For example, I would like to ask the rest of the group how they handle people who want to argue all the time. I think we should all agree on the ten areas we'll talk about, so everyone will enjoy sharing. Do you have some suggestions about topics you'd enjoy talking about? Or, would you like to think about it before telling me what you would like to include?

OWNERSHIP OF THE TOPICS SHOULD BE SHARED!

To your great surprise, you may discover that your opportunities to share Christ in the gatherings does not depend on forcing the topic into spiritual subjects! For example, in one Share Group one of the Type "B" Unbelievers suggested the topic for one evening might be football. One of the Team members said, *"How does that topic help us bring the message of Jesus to the group?* As the discussion developed, one of the Type "B" Unbelievers asked one of the Team,

"Which team are you betting on?"
The Christian replied, "Well, I enjoy sports, but I never bet."
"Really? Don't you even join the betting pool in your office during football season?"
"No. Betting doesn't fit with my lifestyle. You see, I

really don't believe that things happen because of "luck" or "chance." The scriptures teach that God is in charge of His world, and that "luck" just doesn't exist."

Whew! The conversation that followed was handled with great sensitivity and love by the Team. For the first time, the Type "B" Unbelievers were exposed to some very simple basic truths of the Christian life—that we trust in a God who will provide for all our needs. We don't need to "take our chances."

Therefore, don't be too upset about the subjects selected. After all, the purpose of the Share Group is to bond your lives together in a Deep Trust Relationship. *Always remember that!*

Topics which might be considered for "starters" might include: "How do you decide what to do with your time?" "What would you like to be doing five years from now?" Or, "If the doctor told you that you had only six months to live, how would you spend those weeks, and why?"

No matter *what* the topic your Christ-centered values will shape what you say. It's almost as though you can't help but reveal the life you have in Christ!

BEING IN A

SHARE group

IS A WAY OF LIFE!

Read John 4:7-26

Today, we're going to finish this first part of our journey by thinking again about the matter of communication. If you wish, you may review pages 92-97 before reading further. The more you become sensitive to the patterns of communication, as well as the words being spoken, the more the Holy Spirit can use you to win others.

NOTE THE FLOW OF COMMUNICATION BETWEEN JESUS AND THE WOMAN

Consider the patterns of communication described on the chart on page 95. Using your Bible, locate each comment made in the discussion. Then consult the outline on the facing page to learn what type of communication is being used. As you trace the pattern, some interesting facts will be uncovered!

SHARING

Inform

V. 10	—	JESUS
V. 13-14	—	JESUS
V. 17a	—	WOMAN
V. 22-23	—	JESUS
V. 26	—	JESUS

Explore

V. 9	—	WOMAN
V. 11-12	—	WOMAN
V. 25	—	WOMAN

RULE

Persuade

V. 7	—	JESUS
V. 15	—	JESUS
V. 16	—	JESUS

Enforce

GIVE IN

Accommodate

V. 21	—	JESUS

Comply

S-P-L-I-T

Flight

V. 19-20	—	WOMAN

Fight

COUNTDOWN TO SHARE GROUP LAUNCH

WEEK 1: (Date)_____
Develop relationship with first Type "B" Unbeliever

WEEK 2: (Date)_____
Develop relationship with second Type "B" Unbeliever.

WEEK 3: (Date)_____
Develop relationship with third Type "B" Unbeliever.

WEEK 4: (Date)_____
Conduct first "Get-Together."

WEEK 5: (Date)_____
Conduct second "Get-Together."

WEEK 6: (Date)_____
Conduct third "Get-Together."

WEEK 7: (Date)_____
Each Team member invites two Type "B" Unbelievers to attend
10-week Share Group gatherings.

WEEK 8: (Date)_____
Team attends briefing for launching Share Group; Part 2,
"Building Groups" manual is distributed.

WEEK 9: (Date)_____
Team shares in half night of prayer for their ministry.

WEEK 10: (Date)_____
SHARE GROUP LAUNCH

WEEK SEVEN
CELL GROUP EQUIPPING TIME

THE TEAM SHARES...

UP TO 3 MINUTES PER PERSON:
- Share items from your REPORT SHEETS (page 103) with one another.
- Give details of those you will be bringing to the first Share Group meeting.

- **USE THIS PAGE TO RECORD PRAYER REQUESTS ABOUT THE TYPE "B" UNBELIEVERS WHO WILL BE ATTENDING YOUR FIRST SHARE GROUP MEETING . . .**

NAME OF PERSON:	TEAM MEMBER:	REMARKS:

HOW TO HAVE A HALF NIGHT OF PRAYER

LOCATION: One of your homes, where you won't disturb family members.

TIME: Perhaps 10 P.M. TO 2 A.M.? Begin after things "settle down," when you won't be disturbed.

AGENDA: Fellowship

Time of Praise and Worship

Sharing Of Personal Needs

Edification time: praying for one another, building up one another as Christ anoints you for ministry to each other.

One hour of simultaneous prayer time (all praying aloud together!) (Use Outline on opposite page)

Time of Bible study, using Romans 6 as your text.

Brief Break

Sharing of Names and Needs of Type "B" Unbelievers

One to two hours of simultaneous prayer time for them, along with intercession for the Holy Spirit to fill you with His mighty power for your coming ministry

A SCHEDULE FOR PRAYING ONE HOUR

FIRST TEN MINUTES: Worship your Lord.

SECOND TEN MINUTES: Pray for your Pastor(s), your Shepherd, and the members of your Cell Group.

THIRD TEN MINUTES: Pray for your Nation and its Leaders.

FOURTH TEN MINUTES: Pray for the Type "B" Unbelievers in your life.

FIFTH TEN MINUTES: Pray for your family members.

SIXTH TEN MINUTES: Pray for yourself.

Share Group Team Covenant

Knowing that Christ has brought me His peace,
I will offer it to those who have none.
I will help those who are in deep distress,
patiently working with them until they are
able to choose whether they wish to respond
to Christ's unconditional love.
I will respond to all with God's acceptance;
I will not be judgmental
I will always remember that God
allows all things
for His eternal purposes.
I will prayerfully seek to know what,
in each situation, God wants to address—
and be His voice of compassion.
I will earnestly avoid giving simplistic
"solutions" to difficult situations.

Knowing that a Share Group session
may be the turning point for a life,
I covenant to place my commitment
to this ministry at the
very top of my priority list.
As God anoints me, I shall do His work
to expose each Type "B" Unbeliever
to Christ's love, God's grace, and
the Holy Spirit's presence.

_____

_____

_____